F.P. & A.   9/1/81

The Lease/Buy Decision

The Lease/Buy Decision

A Simplified Guide to Maximizing
Financial and Tax Advantages in the 1980s

Pieter T. Elgers
John J. Clark

THE FREE PRESS
A Division of Macmillan Publishing Co., Inc.
NEW YORK

Collier Macmillan Publishers
LONDON

The Free Press
A Division of Macmillan Publishing Co., Inc.
866 Third Avenue, New York, N. Y. 10022

Collier Macmillan Canada, Ltd.

Library of Congress Catalog Card Number: 80-66131

Printed in the United States of America

printing number

1 2 3 4 5 6 7 8 9 10

Library of Congress Cataloging in Publication Data

Elgers, Pieter T
    The lease/buy decision, a simplified guide to
maximizing financial and tax advantages in the 1980's.

    Bibliography: p.
    Includes index.
    1. Industrial equipment leases. I. Clark, John
J., joint author. II. Title.
HD39.4.E43   1980   658.1'5242   80-66131
ISBN 0-02-909470-4

Contents

Preface

Leasing is the fastest growing industry in the United States. Some economists predict that by the end of the next decade over 80 percent of the nation's capital equipment will be acquired under lease agreements—everything from land, factories, and equipment to aircraft, railroad cars, ships, delivery vehicles, and motor cars, as well as a variety of information processing and retrieval systems. However, the trend toward leasing should not lead to the conclusion that it is good for everyone. The decision to lease or own an asset is almost always a "sharp pencil" operation involving financial, accounting, and tax considerations. The businessman, whether he be the lessor or lessee, need not possess the expertise of the public accountant or tax lawyer, but he must know the questions to ask which will enable him to estimate the financial return from the decision at hand.

It is our purpose, first, to discuss the economic variables common to all lease proposals and to show how they work to the advantage or disadvantage of the leasehold parties. Lease negotiations mostly consist of trade-offs between several key variables. How the trade-offs are reached determines the rental payments on the asset. To put the matter another way, rental payments, representing future commitments to pay, are the outcomes of how the parties to the negotiation estimate the future values of economic variables bearing on the arrangement. *A lease document is a forecast of how segments of the economy are expected to perform over the term of the lease: inter-*

est rates, capital equipment costs, maintenance and operating costs, tax legislation, etc.

Secondly, the economic variables must fit into a financial framework to assess the profitability of the proposed lease. Most books on leasing stress the position of the lessee. In establishing the framework for profit estimation, we attempt a more balanced presentation enabling the reader to appreciate the objectives of both the lessor and the lessee. A skilled negotiator places himself in the other fellow's shoes, understands the limits of compromise, and can identify the areas where mutually satisfactory trade-offs may be effected.

Thirdly, the financial framework for lease analysis rests upon cash flows, inflows and outflows. Yet—and this applies to both the lessor and lessee—a lease which meets the criteria of sound financial planning may in the early years detract from the firm's conventional accounting statements based upon historical costs. Accordingly, management must be aware not only of the cash flow effects of leasing but also of the impact of the lease on the company's financial statements. Stockholders and creditors look to the accounting statements in judging the firm's health. We shall have to be aware of accepted accounting practice in the recording of leases. We will also need to discuss Securities and Exchange Commission regulations relating to the disclosure of lease terms.

Fourthly, much of today's interest in leasing arises out of the tax advantages available to lessor and the lessee. Indeed, if we lived in a truly competitive and tax-free environment, it is fair to say that the advantages of ownership would generally prevail over leasing except where the lessor possessed certain economies of scale not available to the lessee. Tax law, therefore, lies at the heart of leasing. Moreover, it is complicated in application and not always consistent with the standards of accepted accounting practice. No lease should be undertaken without clear understanding of its tax status.

Fifthly, tax statutes bear particularly on leveraged leasing. We treat leveraged leasing as a special case not only because of its importance to the economy and the tax provisions which encourage its growth but also because it constitutes an *agreement between three parties rather than the simple lessor-lessee contract.* One or more creditors take their place with the lessor (owner) and the lessee (rentee). Negotiations and trade-offs grow more compliated.

Lastly, each of the chapters contains examples to illustrate the salient points made in the chapter so that the reader can better judge the implications of the financial, accounting, and tax aspects discussed.

As to the presentation of the material, after a discussion of the historical development of the leasing industry, the pros and cons of leasing are surveyed; then follows a discussion of the key variables common to lease negotiations. The types of leases presently utilized are classified according to financial accounting and tax criteria. This leads into a discussion of the presentation of lease arrangements on the firm's accounting statements and the tax advantages and disadvantages of leasing. The subject shifts at this point to a dynamic setting: the negotiation of a lease deal and the estimation of its profitability for the lessor and the lessee. What are the key variables (costs and incomes) to watch in the negotiation? What is the minimum rental acceptable to the lessor? What is the maximum rental the lessee can afford to pay? The complexity of the discussion builds slowly from simple lease negotiation, to the case of the manufacturer who can sell or lease his product, to the inner workings of leveraged leasing. A concluding chapter pulls together the basic rules of leasing and underscores the theme of the book, namely, *that the businessman interested in leasing should make his independent estimate of the proposal's profitability and not rely exclusively on the assessments of his accountant, tax adviser, lawyer, banker, or other interested parties.* There are many advantages to leasing; there are also risks.

Leasing inevitably involves calculations. However, the jargon used and explained is no more than the reader would meet at his bank, filling out his income tax, or making an investment. Leasing also involves formulas. But while we put the appropriate formulas in the text as a matter of information, we used tables in the Appendix to solve the illustrating problems. This expedient reduces all calculations to simply adding, dividing, or multiplying on a hand calculator.

We do not offer a definitive book on leasing—if indeed such be possible in so dynamic an industry. We tender a guideline to the businessman so that he may approach the issues with a certain independence of mind—aware of the pitfalls, knowledgeable about the potential benefits to his company. We include a bibliography of articles which cover various aspects of leasing and implementation in particular industries. Among these selections you may find one approximating your own situation.

The Lease/Buy Decision

CHAPTER 1

The Leasing Industry

Leasing, an ancient practice, emerged as a growth industry in the latter part of the post-World War II period. The U.S. Department of Commerce, Bureau of Domestic Commerce in December 1976 estimated that 15 percent of all capital equipment purchases were made through leasing arrangements and the inventory of capital equipment out on lease would double by 1980. Approximately $16 billion of new capital equipment was leased in 1975, and the annual volume per year thereafter was projected at a 12 to 15 percent rate. In 1977 corporations, governmental bodies, and consumers leased more than $100 billion of equipment. Nor was the leasing boom confined to "big business." In fact, big leasing deals are now declining, while leases of $100,000 to $2 million items are on the rise. In short, leasing is for everyone—for professional people, plain consumers, small businessmen, and the industrial giants. Entry to the game is easy, exits are fast; but it takes savvy to stay in.

The boom in leasing originated in the increasing complexity and cost of capital equipment, changes in tax and banking regulations, and the need to expand capital spending as well as to modernize capital facilities. The consequences of inflation also encourage leasing. For the lessee, a fixed rental becomes easier to carry as the dollar shrinks over time. For example, a 6 percent inflation rate means that every dollar of rental paid today will be worth 75 cents in five years, and in ten years the equivalency will drop to 56 cents. Moreover, in-

1

flation leads to high interest rates, which deter indebtedness but *may, under given circumstances discussed in later chapters, make leasing cheaper.* The trend of interest rates is a crucial variable in assessing the future of leasing.[1]

Historical Development

Yet leasing is not a phenomenon of the postwar environment. Leasing began with Phoenician ship charters 3,000 years ago and has through the centuries to the present time been a major factor in financing maritime operations. The practice passed to the Graeco-Roman world from which Western civilization evolved. The relation of landlord and tenant originated as an outgrowth of the feudal system, under which a serf, the forerunner of the tenant, held or possessed the land of his feudal lord, as distinguished from a freeholder, who owned the land he occupied. These ancient practices set many precedents governing the relationship between the lessor and lessee in the twentieth century.

From the maritime trade, leasing spread to other forms of transportation. Railroads from their inception resorted to leasing arrangements to finance rolling stock and fixed installations. Airlines continue the tradition. The *New York Times* (November 6, 1977) reported:

> In 1963, Pan American World Airways, like much of the smart money, began playing the newest game in high finance. Rather than buying three 707's at $6.64 million per plane, the airline signed a 13-year lease with the embryonic Sally Leasing Company of Greenwich, Connecticut.
>
> It ultimately paid $11.1 million per plane, but at $71,115 a month, that was several hundred dollars a month less than it would have paid for conventional financing at the three percent prevailing interest rate.

Industry followed suit. Computer technology inspired organization of dozens of small leasing companies in the 1960s.

These undercut the computer giant IBM by depreciating the machines over eight to ten years rather than use the four- to five-year standard employed by IBM. Figure 1-1, taken from *The Wall Street Journal*, gives some idea of the range of equipment put up to lease.

Figure 1-1.   Typical Leasing Announcements

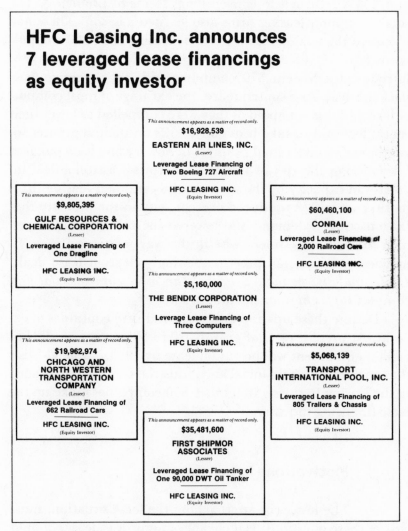

Reprinted with permission of Household Finance Leasing Corp.

But leasing is not all "beer and skittles." It is a game of careful estimation and sharp pencil figuring. Some of the biggest lose. Inflation, for example, works both ways. Pan American had expected the value of the thirteen-year-old 707s would be minimal. Instead, at the conclusion of the lease they had a market value of $4.5 million each and belonged to the Sally Corporation. By 1977 Pan American, United Air Lines, and TWA returned to conventional forms of financing. The small computer leasing firms also learned a lesson. These had absorbed the risk of obsolescence by leasing IBM 360 computers at 10 to 15 percent discounts off the IBM rental rates. IBM introduced a System 370 computer with an attractive lease package deal. As a consequence, the earnings of most computer leasing firms collapsed as they were compelled to lower their rental fees and to take heavy write-offs on their computer inventories. To cite a final example of how leasing is no panacea for avoiding the risk of business enterprise, astronomical increases in capacity by the major cargo container leasing firms in 1977 and 1978 produced overcapacity in the industry that far outstripped demand and lowered the prices of their common stock. Businessmen, wise in the ways of conventional financing, ofttimes fall prey to seemingly clearcut lease deals. *Lease analysis, in fact, is one of the most controversial and complex topics in financial management.*

Despite these ups and downs the industry continues to expand. At present rates of growth, 20 to 30 percent of all U.S. capital equipment will be out on lease by 1980. Table 1-1 lists the top twenty-five financial and industrial companies engaged in the leasing business. In total, 1,800 companies make up the lease financing industry.

Motivations in Leasing

The lessee, in approaching the lease situation, must answer these questions: Is it cheaper to buy or to lease? Should he treat the lease as a form of indebtedness and compare its

Table 1–1.   Top Twenty-five Leasing Companies

Rank	Company
1	U.S. Leasing International
2	Salomon Brothers
3	Citicorp Leasing
4	General American Transportation
5	ITEL Leasing
6	Commercial Credit
7	Dillon Read
8	Kidder, Peabody
9	Morgan Stanley
10	Lehman Corporation
11	C.I.T. Financial
12	Greyhound Leasing & Financing
13	First Chicago Leasing
14	Manufacturers Hanover Leasing
15	Transunion
16	Bankers Leasing
17	Peterson, Howell & Howell
18	Union Bank
19	Goldman, Sachs
20	Ford Motor Credit
21	Halsey, Stuart
22	Chrysler Financial
23	Leasco
24	First Boston
25	Security Pacific

cost to that of borrowing an equivalent sum of money to buy the asset? What is the economic life of the asset and what will it be worth at the end of the lease? Remember, at the end of the lease the asset belongs to the lessor (owner). The *lessor,* on the other hand, must decide whether to sell the asset outright or put it up for lease. If the latter, what rental should he negotiate? The *lessor* also must project the market value at the end of the lease. Both parties necessarily focus on present and future tax rates as well as the trend of interest rates. *Investors* (creditors) in leased equipment must evaluate the credit standing of the lessee, the viability of any guarantees or liens, and the yields desired on their debt certificates in relation to their tax status. The many aspects to the construction of a lease deal led one analyst to conclude:

> The lease-or-buy decision cannot be reduced to a simple formula because of the wide variety of leasing plans available, the different tax treatments which may be accorded them, and the numerous intangible factors that enter the decision.[2]

A few examples will suffice to underscore the point:

1.   Standard Oil of California leases "very large cargo carrier" (VLCC) ships for twenty-five years as an operation peripheral to its business. But some reputable engineers claim the ships will in fact have a useful life of only about sixteen years. If Standard warrants the leasability of the ships, it might face serious legal problems.

2.   Many companies get into the leasing business so that they can show sizable profits to their shareholders while reporting losses on their tax returns. How this is done will be illustrated in subsequent chapters.

3.   Oil and mining companies often make use of leasing simply because oil depletion allowances hold their effective tax rates below those of lessors—the difference being used to reduce the lessee's net cost. The rule of thumb is that a tax-oriented lease can make sense for a lessee if his effective tax rate is below 35 percent.

4.   Industrial corporations (manufacturers) and/or their subsidiaries have joined commercial and investment bankers in financing the leasing boom. U.S. Steel, Eltra, Chrysler Financial, General Electric Credit, and Pepsi Company represent recent entrants. Some companies have entered the field to set up deals that the big banks tend to ignore. This is the case of Greyhound's leasing subsidiary, which handles a variety of leases for regional airlines and equipment leases for medium-sized business.

5.   Leasing companies are highly leveraged. Small changes in total revenues result in greater proportionate changes (plus or minus) in net income. The variability in net

income looks good on the way up, but the added risk can become painfully apparent in periods of economic slowdown. Nonetheless, the leverage feature attracts many investors.

6. Financial managers may prefer to lease equipment rather than purchase the asset. If purchased, the asset becomes part of the firm's capital budget requiring approval of the board of directors. A lease, on the same equipment, may ofttimes be contracted by executive authority alone. The result is expeditiously accomplished and less encumbered by corporate paperwork.

7. Manufacturers can use a lease or sales option to stimulate the distribution of their product. By calculating the point of indifference between leasing and selling (that is, the point that will give the manufacturer the same return whether he leases or sells the asset), the manufacturer can offer a joint purchase or lease package or shift his emphasis from selling to leasing (and vice versa) by lowering the rental or raising the purchase price.

Some Clouds on the Horizon

The postwar leasing boom was in large measure stimulated by tax legislation and inherited accounting practice. Until 1973, firms either did not reveal the existence of leases on their balance sheet or simply noted the existence of a lease without reference to the size of the obligation. Many stockholders learned of the existence of a lease(s) only when the firm encountered financial difficulty.

Accordingly, in 1974 the SEC ruled that leases must be footnoted in financial statements. The firm must add up its future lease obligations, determine the present value of these obligations, and set forth the amounts in a footnote. If as a result earnings would be reduced by more than 3 percent, the reduction must also be disclosed.

The Financial Accounting Standards Board went a step further. Financial Accounting Standard No. 13 (hereafter,

FAS No. 13) requires that leases which are the equivalent of long-term debt must be listed as an obligation on the balance sheet, offset by the capitalized value of the lease as an asset. A problem arising here, however, is that for some companies the inclusion of more debt on the balance sheet will violate existing bond indenture restrictions on debt/equity (D/E) ratios. Table 1-2 projects the impact on debt equity/ratios for a random sample of companies.

FAS No. 13 does not apply to operating leases. Although we shall distinguish between different types of leases in the next chapter, suffice it to say at this point that the rule induces a shift to more expensive operating leases. *Barron's* (February 1979) quotes a U.S. Leasing official as estimating the change-over to an operating lease from a finance lease for a $20,000 minicomputer will cost about 35 percent more over the life of the contract. Yet the official still believes leasing will continue as a popular form of financing. In any event, FAS No. 13 will impact earnings. However, the effect will vary from company to company. Applying the rule to American Airlines' 1976 financial statements would have reduced earnings by 18 percent; in the case of J.C. Penney the reduction would have been 7.4 percent. Whatever the effects are, they will concern principally retailers, fast-food chains, supermarkets, and airlines — all large, publicly owned, and heavy in leasing. Other effects can be envisioned:

> The new D/E ratios may cause creditors to extend less credit, and in some circumstances this may encourage leasing.
> Public utilities may be less enthusiastic about leasing new plants.
> Some hospitals may have to curtail their expansion plans.

Not to be outdone, the IRS has revised its own lease guidelines to insist that a leased facility be usable by another company when the lease expires. It is questionable whether many plants can meet this criterion.

Table 1-2. FAS No. 13 — Random Sampling of Its Impact on Debt/Equity Ratios

Present Value of Leases Greater than 10% of Debt

	Report Date	Equity*	Long-Term Debt	Debt/ Equity	Present Lease Value	Adjusted Debt	% Increase in Debt	Adj. Debt/ Equity
American Airlines	12/76	566.4	416.3	.73	778.0	1194.3	186.9	2.11
Associated Dry Goods	1/77	459.3	97.5	.21	208.0	305.5	213.3	0.67
Atlantic Richfield	12/76	3133.7	2162.1	.69	752.2	2914.3	34.8	0.93
Burlington Northern	12/76	1681.8	927.7	.55	199.6	1127.3	21.5	0.67
Dayton-Hudson Corp.	1/77	442.3	226.3	.51	36.0	262.3	15.9	0.59
Gino's Inc.	12/76	46.1	30.0	.65	126.6	156.5	422.1	3.39
Great Atlantic & Pac. Tea Co.	2/77	471.5	107.6	.23	116.2	223.8	108.0	0.47
Hilton Hotels	12/76	231.0	102.8	.45	46.5	149.3	45.2	0.65
Holiday Inns	12/76	471.6	264.9	.56	55.6	320.5	21.0	0.68
Howard Johnson	12/76	228.6	3.9	.02	182.8	186.7	4652.7	0.92
K-Mart Corp.	1/77	1441.8	210.9	.15	1764.1	1975.0	836.6	1.37
May Department Stores	1/77	563.8	414.3	.73	103.0	517.3	24.9	0.92
McDonald's Corp.	12/76	492.0	496.5	1.01	329.0	825.5	66.3	1.68
Melville Corp.	12/76	217.4	52.5	.24	13.9	66.4	26.5	0.31
Pan American World Airways	12/76	352.2	727.3	2.07	588.7	1316.0	80.9	3.74
Ramada Inns	12/76	126.7	291.2	2.30	30.5	321.8	10.5	2.54
Redman Inds.	3/77	10.4	18.0	1.74	7.8	25.8	43.6	2.49
Safeway Stores	12/76	846.2	102.7	.12	1003.4	1106.1	976.8	1.31
Sears, Roebuck	1/77	5936.9	1563.5	.26	359.0	1922.5	23.0	0.32
Standard Oil Co. (Indiana)	12/76	6146.7	1757.7	.29	520.9	2278.6	29.6	0.37
Texaco	12/76	9002.1	2585.5	.29	905.7	3491.1	35.0	0.39
Woolworth (F. W.)	1/77	983.9	428.9	.44	1054.5	1483.4	245.9	1.51

*Common tangible equity

Source: Oppenheimer & Co. Reprinted by permission.

9

All the same, rules are made to be interpreted and one senses the dire results may be overstated. In the present economy, the leasing industry has a too important function to jeopardize its future.

Summary

Leasing has become a pervasive form of financing capital assets. As with debt instruments and stock, it should not be considered the exclusive province of "big" business. Small and medium-sized business can take equal advantage of lease arrangements. And the contacts are waiting. The leasing industry has 1,800 firms, and your local bank may have a leasing subsidiary.

On the other hand, if there are people waiting to serve you (at a price), it behooves you to study the analysis of leasing. *You must clearly understand your own objectives in assuming a lease vis-à-vis conventional financing and master the jargon of leasing.* If leasing will reduce your firm's cost of financing, lower your tax bill, permit you to acquire more assets than your resources would ordinarily allow, and so on, what are the dollar and cents payouts on these advantages? Don't simply follow the establishment in your industry; joining the crowd is never an acceptable investment policy. Don't let someone else figure the cost of leasing—do it yourself. You may negotiate a better deal or at least feel satisfied that the deal you accept is the best under the circumstances. For this you will have to invest sweat and a pocket calculator (or lease one).

CHAPTER 2

Pros and Cons of Leasing

This and the concluding chapter of the book provide an overview of the potential benefits and possible disadvantages to leasing, from a lessee perspective. Each of the points drawn together in this chapter is developed at some length in later chapters. While there is some risk of oversimplification in any brief statement of lease pros and cons, we believe that this overview provides a useful frame of reference for the detailed discussions to follow.

Pros and Cons of Financial Leases

1. Leases provide off-balance-sheet financing. The accounting rules for reporting leases to investors allow some leases to be omitted from the listing of company assets and liabilities on the balance sheet. Off-balance-sheet financing does not *explicitly* raise the debt/equity ratio and impair the borrowing capacity of the firm. This advantage is likely to be overstated. The lease does appear as a balance sheet footnote, and only a naive loan officer or investment banker would ignore the impact of the lease on the financial ratios of the firm.

2. Lease financing conserves working capital. A lease typically requires no down payment and, unlike a bank loan, no compensating balance. Yet, since it may be argued that leases are merely other forms of debt, bank loan agreements might be arranged to provide funds for the down payment

on asset purchases, and also might be set large enough to cover compensating balance requirements. The basic issue is whether leases provide the financing more cheaply than do other forms of borrowing.

3. The lease assists the process of cash budgeting by permitting accurate projections of cash needs. This would be a desirable feature over short-term finnancing, or debt arrangements where the overall line of credit on interest rates may be renegotiated periodically. There is no clear advantage over long-term financing at an established rate of interest.

4. Leasing allows the company to retain a degree of flexibility in financial activities often lost by resort to debt financing. For example, bank loan indenture agreements sometimes impose onerous restrictions on borrowing firms concerning key financial ratios, profitability requirements, shareholder dividend policies, and other financial actions. Lease agreements, on the other hand, will generally not concede to the lessor the power to impose such restrictions. The lessor's interest is presumed to be secured by the leased asset itself.

5. Internally, leases are often more flexible than borrow and buy. Since leases are often treated as operating rather than capital expenditures, plant managers with some discretion can make lease deals quickly, without going the lengthy capital expenditures route. Of course, this possible advantage from an operating manager's perspective is based on inconsistency in the application of a company's capital expenditure screening devices, *if* in fact the lease is tantamount to a purchase.

Leases may also be seen as more flexible since the lessee is not committed to using the asset throughout its useful life, if the lease is cancelable or includes a sublet privilege. But some lease arrangements may impose *less* rather than *more* flexibility: a noncancelable lease may restrict company actions more than the purchase of an asset with an active secondary market.

6. Leases may be financially less burdensome than conventional forms of debt for firms encountering financial distress. While the default of a single installment on a serial bond may result in the entire principal and interest becoming due and payable, the federal bankruptcy law permits a lessor of real estate to recover only three years' lease payments if the lessee goes into reorganization. Lessors of personal property (everything except land and buildings) do have a claim for the full value of the property subject to proof of damages.

7. There can be tax advantages to leasing. The tax law provisions for rapid write-offs of asset cost, as well as investment tax credits, have contributed to the strong recent interest in leveraged leasing.

Leasing can also be a method of depreciating land. To wit, a firm owning land and buildings can depreciate for tax purposes only the building and its equipment. If, however, the entire holding—land, buildings, and equipment—is sold to a subsidiary or independent corporation and leased back to the seller, the entire rental payment becomes tax deductible. The seller might also enjoy a capital gain tax benefit. Depending upon the circumstances, the sale and leaseback can be an attractive proposal to the financial manager seeking to lower his tax bill and build liquidity.

8. There is also a convenience factor to leasing. The bulk of lease contracts are for equipment worth $50,000 or less: trucks, automobiles, office machines. Unless the lessor can pass onto the lessee economies of scale resulting from access to secondary markets or intensive use of maintenance facilities, such deals frequently offer small savings and are probably more costly than ownership. Their attraction lies in the intangible factor of convenience. If the company had the cash available and could use all the tax advantages of ownership, leasing should offer no financial gain.

9. In many states property taxes are not levied on leased assets, since in a legal sense the lessee does not have physical title to the property.

10. Leasing allows for piecemeal financing of relatively small equipment acquisitions for which debt financing would be impractical. There are scale economies in raising addition-

al funds, so that new debt or equity issues are typically large in dollar amount, and episodic in the life of a business. Over the periods between large flotations of new debt or equity securities, leasing may provide an expedient and relatively efficient means of financing.

11. Leasing is advantageous for firms with low or heavily sheltered earnings because the lessor will be able to pass on the tax savings from ownership to the lessee in the form of a lower lease rate.

12. Leasing protects the company from the risks of equipment obsolescence. This advantage depends upon the lease term being appreciably shorter than the physical life of the asset, and the lessee having the option of renewing the lease at the end of the initial lease term, at predetermined rentals. The risk of obsolescence may be far less for a lessor than for a lessee if the asset has a well-developed secondary market. The economic life of an asset depends upon the firm that uses its services: propeller-driven passenger aircraft continue to serve many regional markets, and the vacuum tubes in older computers continue glowingly to provide for the data processing needs of smaller companies.

Summary

This brief catalog of the potential advantages of leasing arrangements has been tempered throughout by factors which may curtail or even erase the benefits. The importance of these possible benefits varies with the circumstances of the firm, and the astute analyst will recognize cases where various alleged advantages do not apply, or are more or less important to his firm.

It is well to recognize that many of the potential advantages to leasing are *qualitative* in nature and so not easily incorporated into the *quantitative* analysis of lease arrangements outlined in the later chapters. The seasoned analyst keeps in mind that the decisions indicated by qualitative decision tools await leavening by his or her subjective judgments and insights. To be sure, potential advantages such as tax cash flow effects are easily incorporated into the formal evaluations of lease proposals. But perhaps equally important and more qualitative characteristics, such as flexibility of financial or operating decisions, are difficult at best to treat in an analytical way. It is for this reason that we continue to emphasize to the reader in later chapters that an *analytical* solution to the lease/purchase decision is merely the first step in reaching a correct decision.

CHAPTER 3

Key Variables
in Lease Negotiation

There are common variables in all lease negotiations. Some are financial; others concern the legal options available to the parties and their rights and defenses. However, whatever their nature, these variables all have an economic impact which must fit into the framework of lease analysis. It is pertinent at this point, therefore, to discuss and illustrate terminology useful in lease analysis and negotiation. Subsequent chapters will apply the analytical framework to the negotiating position of the lessor and lessee.

Framework of Lease Analysis

Lease analysis is carried through on the basis of cash flows, not accounting numbers. The cash flows will eventually affect the accounting reports: if the lease analysis points to a profitable deal, the economic gain will eventually show up on the accounting statements, albeit perhaps with a time lag.

In cash flow analysis, there are three terms of crucial importance: *present value; internal rate of return;* and *cost of capital.* These terms typify capital budgeting decision making (or long-term asset management), and the *decision to lease or own is a capital budgeting decision.*

Present Value

The term means exactly what it implies. What is the present value today of money payable one, two, ten, etc., years (or fractions of a year) in the future? To arrive at the present value of a given sum of money or a series of cash flows payable over several future periods, we discount the future payments by an appropriate discount rate. In essence, the process does not differ from what happens when the bank discounts your personal note or home mortgage. Let's illustrate the concept. Assume a company could buy a piece of equipment which would reduce *cash* operating costs for five years by $6,000 per period. The equipment would cost $20,000 and the company's cost of financing would run to 8 percent. What is the *net present value* (NPV) of the equipment? The most expeditious way of arriving at the answer lies in using Tables A-1 and A-2 in the Appendix.

Period (t)	Cash Flow (A_t)		Interest Factor (IF)*		Present Value (PV)
1	$6,000	×	.926	=	$ 5,556
2	6,000	×	.857	=	5,142
3	6,000	×	.794	=	4,764
4	6,000	×	.735	=	4,410
5	6,000	×	.681	=	4,086
6	6,000	×	.630	=	3,780
Present value of cash flow savings					$27,738
Less					
Cost of equipment (I)					20,000
Net present value (NPV)					$ 7,738

*From Appendix Table A-2, $1 discounted annually at 8 percent gives the above interest factors (IF). This table assumes cash savings are realized at the end of the year.

Since each year's cash flow is the same (i.e., $6,000), this is termed an annuity. In this case the calculation can be shortened by employing the following formula and using Table A-1 in the Appendix.

$$NPV = A_t \times \sum_{t=1}^{N} \frac{1}{(1+R)^t} - I \qquad (1)$$

= annual cash flow $\times$ annuity factor (Table 1) $-$ I

where:

Σ = means summation
N = total number of periods
t = a particular period (for example, t = 1 indicates payment at end of each period and t = 0, payment at beginning of each period)

Thus

$$NPV = \$6,000 \times \sum_{t=1}^{6} \frac{1}{(1+.08)^t} - \$20,000 \qquad (2)$$

From Table A-1 $\sum_{t=1}^{N} \frac{1}{(1+.08)^t}$ for 6 periods (N = 6) yields an interest factor of 4.623. Therefore

$$
\begin{aligned}
NPV &= \$6,000 \times 4.623 - \$20,000 \qquad (3) \\
&= \$27,738 - \$20,000 \\
&= \$7,738
\end{aligned}
$$

What is the significance of net present value? Briefly, in the above situation it means that the equipment is worth more ($7,738) than its cost to the company. If the company were to invest $27,738 in the equipment ($20,000 + $7,738), then the annual cash saving of $6,000 for six years would provide an 8 percent return on the investment. Given that the equipment costs just $20,000, the excess or net present value is $7,738.

Internal Rate of Return (IRR)

The concept represents the same basic process except that it asks the question, What rate (R) will discount the cash flows

(A_t) to equal the investment (I)? This is found by a process of trial and error using Table A-1 and Formula (1) above. Let's experiment with 18 percent and 20 percent to solve for R.

%	IF	Period Cash Flow (A_t)	Present Value
18%	3.498	$6,000	$20,988
R?	?	$6,000	$20,000
20%	3.326	$6,000	$19,956

$$\frac{\$20,988 - \$20,000}{\$20,988 - \$19,956} = \frac{\$988}{\$1032} \times .02 = .019$$

Then

$$R = .18 + .019 = .199 \quad \textit{internal rate of return (IRR)}$$

and

$$\frac{\$988}{\$1,032} \times (3.498 - 3.326) = \frac{\$988}{\$1,032} \times .172 = .165$$

Then

$$IF = 3.498 - .165 = 3.333 \quad \textit{interest factor}$$

In short, an investment of $20,000 in the equipment will yield the company 19.9 percent. When NPV equals zero, the IRR equals R. Figure 3-1 illustrates the relationship between present value, the discount rate, the number of periods, and the cash flow per period. *Note that the higher the discount rate, the lower is the present value because the present value declines as the required return increases* (Figure 3-1).

Cost of Capital (K)

A firm draws on many types of capital to finance the acquisition of assets: current liabilities, long-term debt, pre-

Figure 3–1.   Relationship Between Present Value
Interest Factors, Interest Rates, and Time

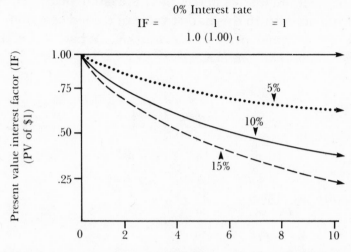

$$IF = \frac{1}{1.0\ (1.00)_t}\ \overset{0\%\ \text{Interest rate}}{=} 1$$

ferred stock, common stock, and retained earnings. Each of
these different sources of capital has a cost. *There is no free
capital.* The firm's cost of capital, accordingly, is *a composite
figure, a weighted average of the costs attached to the types of
capital used by the firm.*

The costs averaged here, however, are not the historical
costs presently embedded in the firm's already outstanding securities (stocks, bonds, and other debt), but rather the cost of
the *next dollar* of debt, preferred stock, and equity. Similarly,
the weights applied to these costs consist of the proportions in
which the firm intends to raise new capital, and not the proportions indicated by the firm's accounting or book values of
debt and equity. To illustrate the point, assume a firm wishes
to raise $100,000 of new capital in the following proportions:

Long-term debt	$15,000
Preferred stock	40,000
Equity (common stock and	
retained earnings)	45,000
	$100,000

The firm's investment banker tells management it can sell new debt *at par* for 10 percent; preferred stock to yield 12 percent; and new common at 15 percent. At the latter yield, new common will not disturb the market value of the old common. The firm is in the 50 percent tax bracket. What is the firm's *marginal cost of capital* (K_{mc})?

Source of of Funds	Amount	Proportions	After-Tax Cost*	Weighted Cost
Long-term debt (K_d)	$ 15,000	.15 ×	.05	.0075
Preferred stock (K_p)	40,000	.40 ×	.12	.0480
Equity (K_E)	45,000	.45 ×	.15	.0675
	$100,000	1.00		K_{MC} = .1230, or 12.3%

*Cost of debt: $K_d(1 - T) = .10(1 - .50) = .05$.

Bear in mind the characteristics of a firm's cost of capital:

1. The cost of capital is always computed on an after-tax basis unless otherwise stipulated. The interest cost of debt is reduced by the fact that interest is tax deductible, while the yield on preferred and equity is already on an after-tax basis.

2. We can also think of the cost of capital as that rate which enables the company to maintain the market value of its outstanding securities. If the company subsequently fails to earn a return on its assets at least equal to its cost of capital, the market value of the securities will decline.

3. A firm's cost of capital divides into two components: (a) a risk-free rate of return usually measured by the yield on U.S. Treasury bills, and (b) a premium for risk determined by the operating and financial risks associated with the firm relative to all other firms and/or risk-bearing securities. Putting it another way, the firm must earn a yield on its assets sufficient to cover the risk-free rate in the market plus the risk premium assigned to it by investor expectations, or the market price on its securities will decline.

4. Since there is a tax deduction for interest, and divi-

dends are subject to double taxation (once when earned by the corporation and again when paid to stockholders), the cost of capital *up to some point* can be successively lowered by adding debt to the capital structure (Figure 3-2). However, at some point further increases in company debt would seem too risky and the firm would attempt to strike a reasonable balance be- tween debt and equity financing—the point would approxi- mate the lowest weighted average cost of capital.

From this point we will use the firm's weighted average cost of new capital (or the marginal cost of capital [K_{mc}] as the discount rate in determining present value (Figure 3-3).

Key Variables in Lease Negotiation

The financial variables common to all lease negotia- tions affect the positions of the lessor and the lessee. Usually, these are not fixed numbers, but subject to the judgment of the parties. The values agreed upon through negotiation de-

Figure 3-2.   The Cost of Capital

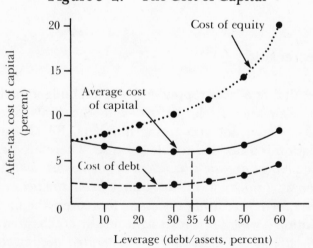

Figure 3-3.   Capital Budgeting Decision Process

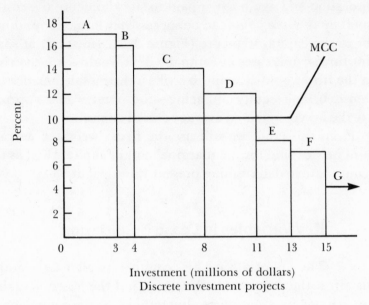

Investment (millions of dollars)
Discrete investment projects

Reprinted with permission of the American College, Bryn Mawr.

termine the eventual rental payments. Key financial variables include:

Depreciation

Recall that a lease represents a capital budgeting decision for the lessor and the lessee. As such, the analysis is based upon *cash flows*, not accounting numbers. Recall, too, that depreciation is a tax-deductible expense. Therefore *depreciation tax savings are an advantage of ownership which is lost when the asset is leased, the advantage being the tax savings to the owner by depreciating the asset.* Moreover, the method of depreciation—whether it is straight line or accelerated depreciation—affects the cash flows. *Accelerated depreciation increases the cash flows (tax savings) in the early years of the*

*project and makes ownership rather than leasing more attract-
ive.* For an illustration of these points, assume:

Cost of equipment	$100,000
Life	10 years
Salvage value	$10,000 at end of 10th year
Marginal tax rate	52%
Discount rate	10%

Case I: Straight Line Depreciation (SL)

Cost of equipment	$100,000
Salvage value	10,000
Amount to be depreciated	$ 90,000

Annual depreciation: $\dfrac{\$90,000}{10} = \$9,000$, or 10% of the depreciable cost of $90,000.

Year	Amount to Be Depreciated	Depreciation (D)	Tax Rate (T)	Tax Savings (DT)
1	$90,000	$ 9,000	.52	$ 4,680
2	90,000	9,000	.52	4,680
3	90,000	9,000	.52	4,680
4	90,000	9,000	.52	4,680
5	90,000	9,000	.52	4,680
6	90,000	9,000	.52	4,680
7	90,000	9,000	.52	4,680
8	90,000	9,000	.52	4,680
9	90,000	9,000	.52	4,680
10	90,000	9,000	.52	4,680
Totals		$90,000		$46,800

In short, the depreciation deduction reduces the firm's tax bill
by $46,800 over the span of the lease. Now note the change
when accelerated depreciation is adopted.

Case II: Double Declining Balance (DDB)

The double declining balance method of accelerated depreciation applies double the straight line rate—in our example, 20 percent—to the adjusted book value (cost less accumulated depreciation) at the start of each fiscal year. Thus DDB calculations ignore salvage value, except that no asset may be depreciated below its salvage value.

Year	Cost of Equipment	Book Value (Cost less Acc. Dep.)	DDB Rate	Depreciation (D)	Tax Rate (T)	Savings (DT)
1	$100,000	—	.20	$ 20,000	.52	$10,400
2	100,000	$80,000	.20	16,000	.52	8,320
3	100,000	64,000	.20	12,800	.52	6,656
4	100,000	51,200	.20	10,240	.52	5,325
5	100,000	40,960	.20	8,192	.52	4,260
6	100,000	32,768	.20	6,554	.52	3,408
7	100,000	26,214	.20	6,554	.52	3,408
8	100,000	19,660	.20	6,554	.52	3,408
9	100,000	13,106	.20	6,554	.52	3,408
10	100,000	6,552	.20	6,554	.52	3,408
Totals				$100,000		$46,800

Observe the tax savings are largely up front under accelerated depreciation compared with the straight line method—that the greatest savings come in the early years.[1]

Case III: Sum of Years Digits (SYD)

Under the SYD method, the rate of depreciation for each year is a fraction: the numerator is the remaining useful life at the beginning of the year and the denominator is the sum of the digits up to the useful life. SYD represents another method of accelerated depreciation, implying that the potential service or productivity of the asset is weighted heavily in the early years of useful life.

Let N designate the number of years in the life of the asset; then a useful shortcut formula is:

$$\text{Sum of the digits} = \frac{N(N+1)}{2}$$

$$= \frac{10(10+1)}{2}$$

$$= 55$$

A fraction of 55 (i.e., 10/55, 9/55, 8/55, etc.) is applied successively each year to the amount to be depreciated (cost of asset less salvage).

Year	Amount to Be Depreciated	Sum of Digits	Depreciation (D)	Tax Rate (D)	Tax Savings (DT)
1	$90,000	10/55	$16,363.63	.52	$ 8,509.08
2	90,000	9/55	$14,727.27	.52	7,658.18
3	90,000	8/55	13,090.91	.52	6,807.27
4	90,000	7/55	11,454.54	.52	5,956.36
5	90,000	6/55	9,818.18	.52	5,105.45
6	90,000	5/55	8,181.81	.52	4,254.54
7	90,000	4/55	6,545.45	.52	3,403.63
8	90,000	3/55	4,909.09	.52	2,552.72
9	90,000	2/55	3,272.72	.52	1,701.82
10	90,000	1/55	1,636.36	.52	850.91
			$90,000.00		$46,800.00

In summary, on a strictly dollar basis the resulting tax savings (DT) are the same for all methods: $46,800.[2] However, since we are dealing with *future* cash flow in choosing a method of depreciation, the discount rate or price of money enters the negotiation and materially alters the lessor's choice. To illustrate:

Year	SL Tax Savings	Discount Rate @ 10% *	Present Value of Tax Savings
1	$4,680	.909	$4,254.12
2	4,680	.826	3,865.68
3	4,680	.751	3,514.68
4	4,680	.683	3,196.44
5	4,680	.621	2,906.28
6	4,680	.564	2,639.52
7	4,680	.513	2,400.84
8	4,680	.467	2,185.56
9	4,680	.424	1,984.32
10	4,680	.386	1,806.48

Total $28,753.92

Add present value of salvage: $10,000 × .386   3,860.00

Present value of SL method $32,613.92

*Discount factors taken from present value tables in the Appendix.

Year	DDB Tax Savings	Discount Rate @ 10% *	Present Value of Tax Savings
1	$10,400	.909	$ 9,453.60
2	8,320	.826	6,872.32
3	6,656	.751	4,998.66
4	5,325	.683	3,636.98
5	4,260	.621	2,645.46
6	3,408	.564	1,922.11
7	3,408	.513	1,748.30
8	3,408	.467	1,591.54
9	3,408	.424	1,444.99
10	3,408	.386	1,315.49

Total $35,629.45

Add present value of salvage: $10,000 × .386   3,860.00

Present value of DDB method $39,489.45

*Discount factors taken from present value tables in the Appendix.

Year	SYD Tax Savings	Discount Rate @ 10% *	Present Value of Tax Savings
1	$8,509.08	.909	$ 7,723.75
2	7,658.18	.826	6,325.66
3	6,807.27	.751	5,112.26
4	5,956.36	.683	4,068.19
5	5,105.45	.621	3,170.48
6	4,254.54	.564	2,399.56
7	3,403.63	.513	1,746.06
8	2,552.72	.467	1,192.12
9	1,701.82	.424	721.57
10	850.91	.386	328.45

Total	$32,799.11
Add present value of salvage: $10,000 × .386	3,860.00
Present value of SYD method	$36,659.11

Allowing for the discount rate on future cash flows, the superiority of the accelerated methods is clearly seen in that the heavy cash flows come in the early periods when the discount rate has a lesser impact on present value. The advantage lies with the DDB method:

Present Value of Depreciation
Tax Deduction

SL method	$32,613.92
DDB method	$39,489.45
SYD method	$36,659.11

Figure 3-4 graphically compares the basic methods of depreciation.

What interest rate should be used in discounting the depreciation tax savings? This is a matter of judgment depending on the probability of a change in the tax rates. Since corporate tax rates do not change frequently, the tax savings from depreciation are not likely to change; that is, the *risk* of a change is low. Assuming this to be the case, the most logical rate would approximate the company's *after-tax cost of debt* (K_d).

Figure 3–4.   Patterns of Annual Depreciation

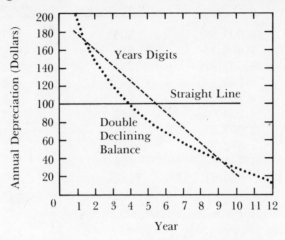

Reprinted with permission of the American College, Bryn Mawr.

We mentioned previously that a company might use straight line depreciation for its accounting and accelerated depreciation for tax purposes. No chicanery is involved; it is a perfectly legal option. How will the accounting statement reflect this management decision? To illustrate, assuming a company adopts the SYD method of accelerated depreciation for tax purposes and SL for accounting purposes, the accounting statements would record the information as follows:

First Year	Accounting Record (SL)	Tax Report (SYD)
Cash sales	$1,000	$1,000
Less		
Depreciation	350	600
Net income before taxes	$ 650	$ 400
Tax rate (.52)	338	208
Earnings after taxes	$ 312	$ 192

Entry:

Tax expense	$312 (under SL)	
Taxes payable		$208 (under SYD)
Deferred tax credits		104 (the difference)

Last Year	Accounting Record (SL)	Tax Report (SYD)
Cash sales	$1,000	$1,000
Less		
Depreciation	350	100
Net income before taxes	$ 650	$ 900
Tax rate (.52)	338	468
Earnings after taxes	$ 312	$ 432

Entry:

Tax expense	$312 (under SL)	
Deferred tax credits	156 (the difference)	
Taxes payable		$468 (under SYD)

Under accelerated depreciation, tax payments are lower in the early years and heavier in the later years. The company's cash flows will be better in the early years and lower in the later years under accelerated depreciation, the difference in effect representing an interest-free loan from Uncle Sam. *The trick is to manage the company's investments so as to take full advantage of this interest-free loan.* All of these considerations impinge on lease negotiations.

Operating Expenses

The operating expenses relating to an asset up for lease constitute a disadvantage to ownership, although the associated costs are reduced by allowable tax deductions. Consequently, if the lessor assumes the operating expenses (repair and maintenance, for example) and does not pass them on fully as higher rentals, this tends to swing the balance in favor of leasing. The lessor may do so if he enjoys economies of scale — that is, if because of the volume of his business, he can maintain and repair the asset at a lower unit cost than the prospective lessee. To induce the lease, he may choose to pass on some of these savings to the lessee in the form of lower rentals. For example, in car rentals, the lessors (Hertz, Avis, Budget, etc.)

accept the costs of repair and maintenance because on a unit basis the volume of business and their facilities bring their costs below those of the individual lessee. Before accepting any lease, investigate your costs in this area. Who pays the operating expenses and the amounts are an important part of the investigation.

Obsolescence

High rates of obsolescence tend to favor leasing and deter ownership. For an asset subject to quick obsolescence (the early computers, for example) acquisition under lease protects the lessee and passes the risk of obsolescence on to the lessor (owner). Conversely, for assets more stable technologically the risk of obsolescence is reduced and this variable becomes less important in negotiations.

Salvage Value

Salvage value is an advantage of ownership lost when the asset is leased. Salvage value (after taxes) belongs to the owner. Accordingly, high salvage values (after taxes) encourage ownership. This advantage to ownership, however, must be tempered by the uncertainty of projecting salvage values five, ten, or twenty years into the future. The uncertainty surrounding salvage values opens a wide area for negotiation. *Since high salvage values mean lower rentals, the lessor will negotiate on the basis of low estimated salvage values. The prospective lessee, on the other hand, will seek lower rentals by projecting higher salvage values.*

Discount Rate

As we have seen in the illustrations on depreciation, lease negotiations involve a forecast of cash flows over the proposed term of the lease. Since the negotiation concerns *future* cash flows, they must be discounted back to the present period at a given rate to obtain the present value of leasing or the present value of ownership. The question then becomes, What discount rate? A high discount rate will mean high rentals, and vice versa. The lessee will negotiate for a low discount rate; the lessor, for a high discount rate.

The proper discount rate is a subject of some controversy in the literature on leasing and depends upon a number of assumptions. Chapters 6 and 7 pick up the threads of this discussion in greater detail. Suffice it to say at this point that the lessor and lessee may have different costs of capital or costs of debt capital or view the lease differently than other debt.

Timing of Rental Payments

Rents can be paid monthly, quarterly, annually. *When they are paid affects the amount of the rentals.* If the rentals are paid in advance (at the beginning of a period), the rental amount will be lower; if they are paid at the end of the period, the rentals will be higher. Obviously, the timing of rental payments is a corollary of present value analysis and the selection of a discount rate.

Tax Factors

The major tax factors in the decision to lease or buy an asset are discussed in Chapter 5. Broadly these include:

1. *Investment tax credit.* The owner of the asset is allowed a credit against income taxes equal to 10 percent of the cost of the property placed in service during the tax year. The full 10 percent is allowed for property with a useful life of at least seven years; two-thirds of 10 percent for property with a life greater than four years; and one-third of 10 percent for property with a life greater than two years. The investment tax

credit does not reduce the cost basis of the asset for purposes of tax depreciation. *The investment tax credit is an advantage of ownership which is lost when the asset is leased.*

2. *Depreciation.* See above.

3. *Capital gains and losses. Depreciable assets do not fall within the IRS definition of a capital asset and thus do not receive the favorable treatment accorded capital assets.* Capital assets include all business property except inventories, real estate, depreciable property used in business, and certain other items.

4. *Operating expenses and rental payments are fully tax deductible.*

5. *Effective tax rates. Differences in the effective tax rates of the lessor and lessee are of special importance in motivating leveraged leases and other tax shelter arrangements.* A lease can generate tax savings if one party (the lessee) has tax deductions but not the income to take advantage of such deductions and the other (the lessor) has the income but lacks deductions to minimize the tax impact.

6. *Existence of prior tax losses. The existence of prior tax losses may vitiate the use of investment tax credits and accelerated depreciation deductions, thus encouraging leasing rather than ownership.*

Some Legal Variables

A good rule for the businessman to follow is, Don't attempt to *draft* your own lease. With appropriate "homework" you may negotiate the general economic terms of the lease, but do not take on the burden of fashioning the lease document. A lease not only is a credit instrument but must comply with the relevant tax and accounting guidelines, the provisions of the Uniform Commercial Code, the common law, Securities and Exchange Commission regulations, and the bankruptcy law. In short, you need a lawyer *experienced in lease negotiations*—not just any lawyer. Also, don't rely on standardized lease forms. Simply that something is in writing does not mean that it complies with public policy or that it will be (or has been) interpreted in the manner you anticipated. Nonetheless, there are a few check points—among very many —that you might wisely bear in mind.

Types of Leases

Make sure the lease meets the criteria for leases spelled out in Chapter 2; otherwise you may end up with a conditional bill of sale and not a lease. The former carries a different set of legal rights and obligations.

Duration of Lease

The parties to the negotiation determine the duration of the lease. However, in long-term leases the lessee may have a right of early cancellation upon payment of a reasonable premium or an option to purchase the asset at fair market value prior to the termination of the lease. This constitutes a desirable feature for the lessee if the lease is negotiated during a period of abnormally high interest rates.

Amount of Periodic Rentals

As a corollary to the above, some lessors negotiate for an increase (or decrease) in rentals if interest rates increase (or decrease). On the other hand, most leases provide for a fixed schedule of rentals over the term of the lease. However, in certain industries—construction, for example—the schedule of lease payments may be higher during peak seasons than at other times.

Dragnet Clause

Lease obligations are sometimes secured by a pledge of outside collateral.

Disclaimer of Warranties

Lessors frequently attempt to insert a disclaimer of warranties. However, even in the presence of a specific written disclaimer, the lessor *may* be held to implied warranties regarding the fitness and merchantability of the asset in a true lease. The wording of any disclaimer should, therefore, be clear, specific, and prominently displayed in the lease. It is for the lessee to negotiate a *quid pro quo* for accepting a disclaimer of warranty.

Also, if the lessee should incur increased tax liability or have to revise his financial statements because the transaction is held to be an installment sale rather than a true lease, the lessor may be held liable for damages arising from breach of an implied warranty of leasability. The lessor, however, can protect himself with an express written disclaimer.

Waiver of Defenses against Lessor's Assignee

If the lessor contemplates assigning the lease to a third party or pledging it as collateral, he will seek to insert a clause providing that on notice of the assignment or pledge, the lessee waives all defenses and claims under the lease against the assignee. The lessee counters by reserving all his rights against the lessor.

Risk of Loss, Insurance, and Redelivery

Generally, the lessee is not obligated to continue his payments after loss or destruction of the equipment unless the catastrophe results from the lessee's negligence or improper use of the equipment. Conversely, the terms of the lease may obligate the lessee to continue paying the rentals, thus becoming in effect the insurer of the property.

In order to underscore the existence of a true lease, the lessee should have the specific obligation to return the equipment to the lessor at the conclusion of the lease at a designated location chosen by the lessor. The lessor should also bear responsibility for any damage to or depreciation of the equipment not resulting from normal wear and tear.

Use of Leased Equipment

The lease should specify all limitations on the use of leased assets. Ambiguity here is often a fruitful source of litigation.

Reclamation in Bankruptcy Proceedings

Generally, in a Chapter XI proceeding, the Federal Bankruptcy Act requires the lessee to continue making the lease payments or the property may be reclaimed by the lessor. But there is some case law allowing exceptions with which your attorney should be familiar.

In a Chapter X proceeding, the Bankruptcy Act provides that an express covenant in a lease terminating the transaction on bankruptcy is enforceable. The most notable cases involve aircraft, ships, and railroad rolling stock. However, the lease should contain a specific provision relating to this contingency.

Default, Acceleration, and Damages

A lessor may not accelerate all unpaid rents upon default by the lessee unless the lease has an acceleration clause. The lease, conversely, should clearly define the meaning of default. Unless otherwise provided in the lease, the acceptance of late payments may be deemed a waiver of similar subsequent defaults.

As to the remaining unpaid rents, the courts have generally upheld a liquidated damages clause which provides that the measure of damages upon default by the lessee is the difference between (1) the present value of the remaining unpaid rentals, less the cost of unperformed covenants of the lessor under the lease, and (2) the fair market rental value of the equipment for the remaining term, discounted to present value. The liquidated damages may be modified in particular cases by other variables.[3]

Summary

Leasing is always a "sharp pencil" operation: that is, in a great many cases the difference between owning and leasing may be only a few dollars. Consequently, hard bargaining on the above variables can swing the balance in either direction. Within the bargaining process, therefore, it is important to both the lessor and lessee not only to estimate carefully the limits on their own positions but also, to the fullest extent possible, to estimate the limits of the other party's position. This will at least help to establish a realistic bargaining area. For example, the lessee will bargain for lower rentals. He can probe the lessor's stance more intelligently if he understands the impact of accelerated depreciation, investment tax credit, timing of the rental payments, the discount rate, salvage values, etc., on the size of the rental payments. The lessor bargains for higher rentals and will take a contrary position on these variables. Finally, with the dollar advantage to lease or own frequently so thin (especially in short-term leases), the lessee may choose to decide on purely subjective grounds, namely, the convenience of ownership and the lesser likelihood of legal hassles concerning the proper use of the leased property.

Lessees too often rely on the supposed expertise of the lessor — a good way not to achieve your objective. Similarly, while you will need the services of an experienced lease attorney and accountant, make sure you understand the implications of each covenant and the potential cost to you the lessee (or lessor). We have given you some of the questions to raise; do not act in haste on the answers you receive.

CHAPTER 4

Types of Leases and Financial Accounting Implications

Recently the Financial Accounting Standards Board (FASB), the rule-making body for corporate financial accounting reports, issued a long-awaited and highly debated set of rules for reporting leases in financial statements. Basically, the FASB provides a set of *classifications* for lease agreements, for both lessors and lessees. In turn the classification of a lease determines how it will be reported in the financial statements.

The key issue in accounting for leases is whether companies can still arrange "off-balance-sheet financing" via leasing of assets. A major purported advantage of leases from a lessee standpoint is the ability to acquire the use of equipment for extended periods, without entering the leased equipment on the balance sheet as an asset and without entering the future lease payment obligations as a liability. Since it is widely assumed that investors, lenders, and others define company debt in terms of the amounts reported in the company balance sheet, the ability to relegate information about lease financing to the footnotes of the financial statements has been seen as a substantial advantage. This belief apparently persists: subsequent to the passage of the new set of rules (FAS No. 13), many leasing firms have begun to advertise their ability to create "FAS No. 13 Financial Leases," i.e., leases which still manage to qualify for "off-balance-sheet" treatment. Since such leases are often *less* attractive when evaluated from a purely financial perspective (using techniques such as those provided in Chapters 6 and 7), there seems to be a prevailing belief among many prospective lessees that bankers and investors are naive users of balance sheet data.

FAS No. 13 establishes criteria for classifying various kinds of leases, and a set of reporting standards for each class. Broadly, for the lessee all leases are either (1) capital leases or (2) operating leases. *A lease possessing any one of a set of very explicit criteria is a capital lease, which means that the lease payments, discounted for interest, must be "capitalized" as an asset and also shown as a liability on the balance sheet.* The criteria are written so as to include a substantial majority of all long-term lease arrangements, and will be described below. All other leases are treated as operating leases. With an operating lease a user acquires use of an asset for a fraction of its useful life, and the lessor bears the risk of ownership. For accounting purposes operating leases do not appear on the balance sheet as assets or liabilities and the lease payments are interpreted simply as rental expenses.

In the case of a lessor, the new accounting standard distinguishes between four lease types: (1) sales-type leases, (2) direct financing leases, (3) leveraged leases, and (4) operating leases. Broadly, sales-type leases, direct financing leases, and leveraged leases from the lessor's standpoint usually qualify as capital leases for the lessee, though there are important exceptions. Likewise, operating leases are for the most part classified the same way by lessors and lessees. The exception will become clearer as we provide a fuller definition of each lease type in the following pages.

Financial Accounting Classifications of Leases[1]

From the standpoint of the *lessee*, accountants must classify leases as either (1) capital leases, or (2) operating leases. Capital leases meet *one or more* of the following criteria:

1. The lease transfers ownership of the property to the lessee by the end of the lease.
2. The lease contains a bargain purchase option.
3. The lease term is equal to 75 percent or more of the estimated economic life of the leased property.
4. The present value at the beginning of the lease term of the minimum lease payments equals or exceeds 90 percent of the fair value of the leased property to the lessor at the inception of the lease (over and above any related investment tax credit retained by the lessor).

Usually the lessee will compute the present value of the minimum lease payments using his incremental borrowing rate, though in some cases it may be appropriate to use the lessor's implicit rate of return on the lease, if known by the lessee.

All leases meeting *none* of the four criteria posed above for capital leases are classified as operating leases.

To show the accounting requirements imposed by the criteria for capital leases, consider the following example.

Assumptions:

Lessor's cost of equipment (assumed equal to fair market value)	$50,000
Estimated economic life of equipment	5 years
Lease term	30 months
Rental, paid at beginning of each month	$1,350
Residual value estimated at end of lease term	$20,000
Lessee's incremental borrowing rate	10½%
Lessor guarantees the residual value of $20,000.	

Given these assumptions, the minimum lease payments are $60,500, computed as follows:

Minimum rental payments over lease term
($1,350 × 30 months)	$40,500
Residual value, guaranteed by lease	20,000
	$60,500

This package of minimum cash flows would provide the lessor with an implicit rate of return of 1.003 percent per month, or 12.036 percent per year (for the mechanics of calculating implicit rates of return by lessors, see Chapter 7).

At this point, the lease is measured against the four criteria for capital leases described earlier. In this case:

1. Not met: the lease does not transfer ownership by the end of the lease term.
2. Not met: there is no bargain purchase option.
3. Not met: the lease term is 30 months, or 2½ years, while 75 percent of the property's useful life would be 45 months, or 3¾ years.
4. Met: therefore, the lease is a capital lease.

In this case, the lessee computed the present value of the minimum lease payments using his incremental borrowing rate of 10½ percent. This amount (determined using the basic tools of present value analysis presented in Chapter 6) is $51,200. Since the fair value of the property at the inception of the lease is just $50,000, it is clear that the present value of the minimum lease payments exceeds the 90 percent test.

The capital lease would be recorded by the lessor, so that assets and liabilities would increase by $50,000 upon the signing of the lease. Likewise, the income statements would reflect charges for (1) depreciation expense for the use of the leased asset, and (2) interest expense for the implicit interest on the lease obligation (in this case, about 12 percent per year). Generally, for leases with level payments, the total depreciation and interest expenses will substantially exceed the annual rentals in the earlier years of the lease agreement, and the situation will reverse in the later years of the lease.

From the lessor standpoint, there are four lease types, which can be described as follows:

Sales-type Lease

These arrangements provide a profit or loss to the lessor as a manufacturer or dealer, and are normally found where manufacturers or dealers use leases as a means of manufacturing their products. In effect, the lease agreement has two distinct elements. First, there is a sale of the leased asset, and the lessor earns a profit or loss on this transaction equal to the difference between the cost of the leased asset and the present (discounted) value of the rents to be received. Second, the lessor is extending financing to the lessee (or purchaser) of the asset, and so earns interest income over the life of the lease.

Direct Financing Lease

Leases in this category meet at least one of the criteria listed above for capital leases, and do *not* provide a manufacturer or dealer profit or loss at inception.

Leveraged Leases

These are a special form of direct financing lease, and involve the following features: (1) at least three parties are involved—a lessee, a long-term creditor, and a lessor; (2) the financing provided by the long-term creditor has no claim upon the general credit of the lessor (such debt is termed non-recourse); and (3) the lessor's net investment declines during the earlier years of the lease term, rises again in the later years, and is liquidated by the final lease payment. (Chapter 8 provides detailed descriptions of leveraged lease arrangements and shows methods for their financial evaluation. This chapter will develop the method of accounting for such leases, but does not directly consider the issue of financial benefit.)

Operating Leases

These are all other leases.

To illustrate the accounting for leases by lessors, let us return to the earlier lease example. Since in that case the lease arrangement met one of the criteria listed for capital leases and did *not* provide a manufacturer or dealer profit at inception, the lease is a direct financing lease. Upon signing, the lessor would record the following:

dr	Minimum lease payments receivable $60,500	
	cr Equipment	$50,000
	cr Unearned income	$10,500

Note that no profit is recognized at the inception of the lease; the unearned income will be gradually taken into earnings as interest income, over the life of the lease. In effect, the lease is considered as an investment in a financial security, with financial (interest) income being the sole element of profit to the lessor.

The situation is only slightly different in the case of a sales-type lease. For example, assume in the above case that the *cost* of the equipment to lessor is only $40,000 and all other facts remain the same. In this situation the lessor would realize a profit upon signing the lease equal to the difference between cost ($40,000) and fair value at the inception of the lease ($50,000), or $10,000. After this profit is recognized, the remaining interest income is spread over the life of the lease, as before.

For leveraged leasing, the lessor's accounting requirements are considerably more elaborate, and include the following elements:

1. The lessor is to record his investment in a leveraged lease *net* of the nonrecourse debt. The lessor's continued investment in a leveraged lease is determined by combining all of the following amounts:

a. Rentals receivable, after subtracting the portion of the rental which will be applied to paying off the principal and interest on the nonrecourse debt.

b. Any amount receivable from the government for the amount of the investment tax credit on the leased asset.

c. The estimated residual value of the leased asset.

d. Unearned and defined income relating to the lease arrangement. Usually this consists of interest income to be received over the lease term, and investment tax credits to be allocated to income over the lease term.

2. Since the lessor's pretax income on his financial accounting statements is likely to differ from his taxable income, there will be additional deferred tax debits and credits, and these will also serve to increase or decrease the lessor's net investment.

3. In most cases, the above definitions of net investment will lead to three separate phases over the life of the lease. In the first phase the lessor's net investment is positive and declining; in the second phase the net investment is *negative*; and in the third and final phase the net investment is positive and rising, until liquidated at the end of the lease. In general, income on the leveraged lease will be prorated to each year

based on the amount of net investment in that year; during phase 2, when net investment is negative, no income will be recorded.

In order to illustrate the financial accounting for leveraged leases, consider the following case:[2]

Cost of leased asset	$1,000,000
Lease term	15 years
Rental, payable on *last* day of year	$90,000
Residual value, 1 year after lease ends	$200,000
Lessor's equity investment	$400,000
Debt financing, nonrecourse at 9%	
Principal	$600,000
Annual installments	$74,435
Investment tax credit (10%)	$100,000
Depreciation for tax purposes (the most beneficial methods are reflected in this example; see Chapters 3 and 5 for further discussion)	
Salvage value for tax purposes	$100,000
Lessor's tax rate (federal and state)	50.4%

The first step is to prepare a year-by-year cash flow analysis. In each year, the annual cash flow is computed as follows:

Initial investment (usually paid at inception of lease)

Plus: Investment tax credit received (usually in the first year of the lease)

Plus: After-tax amount of rentals (depreciation and interest expenses are deducted in computing the tax to be paid on the rental income)

Less: Debt payments (principal and interest)

Plus: Residual value, after tax (usually in the final or subsequent year after end of lease)

Table 4-1 shows the calculation of the annual and cumulative cash flows, as defined by FAS No. 13. Note the following:

1. The cumulative cash flow is negative at first, reflecting the lessor's 40 percent equity; by the fifth year the cumulative cash flow is positive, due mainly to the investment tax credit, and to the tax shields created by the large deductions for interest and depreciation in the early years of the lease.

In the later years the cash flows again become negative, owing to large tax payments as the depreciation tax shields are exhausted. At the end of the lease term, after the residual value (net of tax effects) has been realized, the cumulative cash flows are again positive.

While it is reassuring to note that this lease arrangement provides a net positive cash inflow, it should be recognized that the timing of the cash flows is equally as important as their amounts. It is quite possible that leases with *negative* cumulative cash flows will be economically sound, if the cash inflows are predominantly in early years and the cash deficits predominantly in later years. This point will be demonstrated in the discussion of present value concepts in Chapter 6.

2. The total cumulative cash flow ($116,601 in Table 4-1) is allocated to income over the life of the lease in proportion to the lessee's net investment at the beginning of each year. If the lessor has a *negative* investment in any year, then *no* income is allocated to that year.

Since investment tax credits provide a major part of the *accounting* income from a leveraged lease, the procedure for allocating income required by the FASB causes the investment credit to be allocated over the lease term. The point is worth noting, since generally the income effect of investment credits can be taken into income immediately upon purchase of the assets, for transactions other than leveraged leases.

3. In the example shown in Table 4-1, lease income is computed to be 8.647 percent of the unrecovered investment at the beginning of each year. This percentage must be obtained by trial and error, since no income is allocated to years

Table 4-1. Cash Flow Analysis by Years

Year	(1) Gross Lease Rentals and Residual Value	(2) Depreciation (for Income Tax Purposes)	(3) Loan Interest Payments	(4) Taxable Income (Loss) (Col. 1-2-3)	(5) Income Tax Credits (Charges) (Col. 4 × 50.4%)	(6) Loan Principal Payments	(7) Investment Tax Credit Realized	(8) Annual Cash Flow (Col. 1-3+5-6+7)	Allocated to Investment	Allocated to Income*	Lessor's Net Investment at Beginning of Year
Initial investment	—	—	—	—	—	—	—	($400,000)	—	—	—
1	$ 90,000	$ 142,857	$ 54,000	($106,857)	$ 53,856	$ 20,435	$100,000	169,421	$ 134,833	$ 34,588	$ 400,000
2	90,000	244,898	52,161	($207,059)	104,358	22,274	—	119,923	96,994	22,929	265,167
3	90,000	187,075	50,156	($147,231)	74,204	24,279	—	89,769	75,227	14,542	168,173
4	90,000	153,061	47,971	($111,032)	55,960	26,464	—	71,525	63,488	8,037	92,946
5	90,000	119,048	45,589	($ 74,637)	37,617	28,846	—	53,182	50,635	2,547	29,458
6	90,000	53,061	42,993	($ 6,054)	3,051	31,442	—	18,616	18,616	—	($ 21,177)
7	90,000	—	40,163	$ 49,837	($ 25,118)	34,272	—	($ 9,553)	($ 9,553)	—	($ 39,793)
8	90,000	—	37,079	52,921	($ 26,672)	37,357	—	($ 11,108)	($ 11,108)	—	($ 30,240)
9	90,000	—	33,717	56,283	($ 28,367)	40,719	—	($ 12,803)	($ 12,803)	—	($ 19,132)
10	90,000	—	30,052	59,948	($ 30,214)	44,383	—	($ 14,649)	($ 14,649)	—	($ 6,329)
11	90,000	—	26,058	63,942	($ 32,227)	44,378	—	($ 16,663)	($ 17,382)	719	$ 8,320
12	90,000	—	21,704	68,296	($ 34,421)	52,732	—	($ 18,857)	($ 21,079)	2,222	25,702
13	90,000	—	16,957	73,043	($ 36,813)	57,478	—	($ 21,248)	($ 25,293)	4,045	46,781
14	90,000	—	11,785	78,215	($ 39,420)	62,651	—	($ 23,856)	($ 30,088)	6,232	72,074
15	90,000	—	6,145	83,855	($ 42,263)	68,290	—	($ 26,698)	($ 35,532)	8,834	102,162
16	200,000	100,000	—	100,000	(50,400)	—	—	149,600	137,694	11,906	137,694
Totals	$1,550,000	$1,000,000	$516,530	33,470	($ 16,869)	$600,000	$100,000	$116,601	$400,000	$116,601	

*Lease income is recognized as 8.647% of the unrecovered investment at the beginning of each year in which the net investment is positive. The rate is that rate which when applied to the net investment in the years in which the net investment is positive will distribute the net income (net cash flow) to those years.

Source: Abridged from FAS No. 13, Appendix E, Exhibits 1 and 2.

of *negative* investment, and the amount of profit recognized is included in the *definition* of net investment (as shown earlier). This requires a trial-and-error approach to computing the earnings percentage, and usually justifies using a computer program to calculate the correct rate.

  4. *The manner in which financial accountants define leveraged leases, allocate net income to the time periods of the lease, and compute the lessor's net investment at the beginning of each period are each quite different from the procedures required by the IRS, which are detailed in Chapter 5.* It is possible that leveraged leases for accounting purposes will not even qualify as true leases for income tax purposes, given the entirely separate sets of criteria written into the tax laws.

  From the analyses of cash flows and allocations of income developed in Table 4-1, the following accounting entries would be made by calculation of present value of rentals receivable:

Rentals receivable (15 × $90,000)	$1,350,000
Less: Loan principal payment	($600,000)
Loan interest payments	($516,530)
	$ 233,470

And the financial accounts would be affected as follows, upon negotiating the leveraged lease:

dr	Rentals receivable	$233,470
dr	Investment tax credit receivable	$100,000
dr	Estimated salvage value of lease assets	$200,000
	cr Cash	$400,000
	cr Unearned income (the combined totals of columns 4 and 7 in Table 4-1)	$133,470

Tax versus Accounting Classifications of Leases

  The tax law concerning leases is very complicated, and we have provided a general summary of the more important tax implications in Chapter 5. For the present, it is well to recognize that there exists very little parallel between the criteria used by the IRS and those used by the FASB in defining leases. For tax purposes the central question is whether a *true* lease exists, or whether the purported lease arrangement is in substance a conditional sales contract. Upon this basic distinction rests a broad set of tax consequences, discussed in Chapter 5.

Financial Analysis v. Accounting Classifications of Leases

Broadly, the question of concern to financial analysts is the effect of lease arrangments upon the amount, timing, and riskiness of future cash flows to lessor and lessee. At the extreme, a lease agreement which irrevocably obligates the lessee to pay a fixed series of payments over a definite lease term would be viewed as the purchase of an asset's services and the incurrence of long-term serial repayment debt. The leased asset would appear in calculations of the firm's return on assets employed, and the lease obligation would be included in calculations of the lessee's total debt burden, financial leverage ratios, and so on. Conversely, an agreement to rent an asset's services, which may be readily canceled without penalty by either party to the lease, would be viewed as similar to any other of the lessee's variable operating expenses, and so would be omitted from assessments of return on assets, total indebtedness, financial leverage, and so on. Of course, most lease arrangements fall between these two extremes. Yet it has not been necessary for financial analysts to construct a set of rigid criteria to unambiguously classify leases into one type or another. The tools of financial analysis are readily adapted to suit different patterns of cash flows, and to make suitable allowances for differential riskiness. Yet the financial analyst *will* be concerned with how a lease is classified under IRS and FASB reporting requirements, since these classifications may affect the firm's cash flows.

Capital Leases v. Operating Leases: Much Ado About Nothing?

In the years of often sharp debate preceding the FASB's new set of rules for reporting leases, there were frequent dire predictions that such charges would hurt the credit worthiness of companies that leased equipment, thereby inflating their financing costs and depressing the prices of their shares. Such a view rests upon the idea that investors and lenders take a myopic view of financial accounting numbers and systematically disregard other sources of information such as the explanatory footnotes included in the accounting reports. Companies have long been required to include in the details provided with their accounting reports a full description of the cash flow consequences of significant lease contracts, so the major impact of the FASB's action is to move such information up to the body of the main financial statements. For the most part, this is not *new* information; only the geography of its disclosure has changed.

Many security analysts predicted little or no market impact from the new rules, arguing that the information they call for is already known to investors, so that security prices already reflect the consequences of leases. And a number of research studies subsequent to FAS No. 13 bear out the point. Researchers have been unable to detect any important stock price reactions for companies affected by the new rules. It also appears that the *riskiness* of stock prices reflected the impact of leases *prior* to the new reporting requirements. On the other hand, bond indenture agreements and other debt covenants often define limits on company indebtedness and various key financial ratios as reported in the company's financial statements. In these cases, merely cosmetic changes affecting the geography of lease disclosure *may* cause violation of these restrictions, with consequences for the cost and availability of financing.

CHAPTER 5

Tax Regulations Pertaining to Leasing

Federal income tax consequences figure prominantly in all business decisions, and leasing is no exception. In fact, if it were not for income tax advantages, leasing would rarely be preferred to purchases of assets. This chapter reviews those aspects of the federal income tax laws with potentially important effects on the analysis of lease profitability.

Generally, in order for a lease to offer tax advantages, there must be some *difference* in the tax status of lessor and lessee. A "yes" answer to any of the following questions suggests the potential for a profitable lease arrangement:

1. *Do the lessor and lessee have different effective tax rates?* If so, a lease may permit the higher-rate taxpayer to defer tax payments to a later year.
2. *Is either party (lessee or lessor) unable to fully utilize available investment tax credits?* The tax law is flexible enough to allow investment credits to be used by *either* the lessor or the lessee.
3. *Does the potential lessee have a history of operating losses?* If so, he may be unable to benefit fully from fast write-offs of asset cost (accelerated depreciation). A lessor who is able to utilize such benefits may pass on a portion of the savings to the lessee via lower rental charges.

In order to evaluate the importance of investment tax credits and accelerated depreciation on the analysis of leases, it is well to begin with a more detailed explanation of these tax incentives.

Investment Tax Credits

Generally, the federal government subsidizes 10 percent of qualified corporate investment, in the form of an investment credit. When a corporation purchases new, tangible, depreciable property with a life of eight years or more, 10 percent of the cost of such property can be deducted from the company's tax liability. There are several important features:

1. The property must have an estimated useful life of at least eight years to qualify for the full credit. A partial credit is allowed for shorter-lived assets (e.g., one-third credit for property with a life of three to four years, and two-thirds credit for property with a life of five to seven years).
2. Only new, tangible, depreciable property is qualified for the credit, *excluding* buildings and their structural components.
3. The amount of investment credit is limited in any given year to 100 percent of the tax liability up to $25,000, and 50 percent of any excess.
4. Any unused portion of the investment credit may be carried over to other tax years, to offset the taxes otherwise payable in those years. The carryover period extends back three years and forward seven years, so that the investment credit for assets purchased in 1980 might be carried back as far as 1977 and forward until 1987.
5. The investment credit does not reduce the depreciable cost of an asset for tax purposes: the full cost of

the asset (before subtracting the investment credit), less any estimated salvage value, may be expenses on the company's tax return over the asset's useful life.

In order to illustrate the effects of the investment credit, consider the following case:

First Company is considering the purchase of an asset for $750,000, with an estimated useful life of nine years and salvage value of $30,000. Before considering the investment credit, First Company reports taxable income of $350,000, and is taxed at 40 percent.

Analysis: If the asset is *not* purchased, First Company must pay taxes of $140,000 (or $350,000 at 40 percent). If the asset *is* purchased, First Company must pay taxes of $65,000, computed as follows:

$140,000	tax on $350,000 @ 40%
75,000	investment credit (10% of $750,000)
$ 65,000	tax due

It is also necessary to check the *limitations* on the investment credit:

$ 25,000	100% of tax liability up to $25,000
57,500	50% of tax liability in excess of $25,000 (or $140,000 − $25,000 = = $115,000; $115,000 @50% = $57,500)
$ 82,500	total limitation

In this case the limitation ($82,500) is greater than the investment credit ($75,000), so the full credit may be used to reduce the current year's taxes.

Now let us change the facts in the case, to a situation where First Company is unable to use the investment tax credit, either currently or within the carryover period. This sets the stage for a profitable lease arrangement: a prospective lessor who is able to fully utilize the investment credit might pass on the benefit to First Company in the form of lower rentals. To illustrate this point, we will determine the maximum amount of *reduction* in annual lease payments that could be offered by a lessor who is able to use the $75,000 investment credit.

A prospective lessor would evaluate the effect of the $75,000 investment tax credit on the *after-tax* rentals as follows (since the investment credit is a direct reduction of the lessor's tax liability, there is a $75,000 tax effect; to be consistent, we must deal with after-tax lease payments and then convert these to before-tax payments as shown below):

$$\begin{matrix} \text{Present value of after-} \\ \text{tax investment credit} \end{matrix} = \begin{matrix} \text{present value of after-} \\ \text{tax reduction in} \\ \text{lease payment} \end{matrix} \qquad (1)$$

$$\$75,000 = L \times \sum_{t=1}^{N} 1/(1 + K_{mc})^t$$

where L is the after-tax lease payment, and N is the number of years in the lease. Then, assuming that the lessor is taxed at 40 percent, the lease term is nine years, and the lessor's after-tax cost of capital is 12 percent, we use the present value factor shown in Appendix Table A–1 and solve for the after-tax effect on the lease payment, L:

$$\$75,000 = L \times \sum_{t=1}^{9} 1/(1 + 12)^t$$

$$\$75,000 = L \times 5.328$$

$$L = 14,077$$

Since we have determined that the after-tax lease payment can be reduced by $14,077, and the tax rate is 40 percent, the before-tax effect is:

$$\begin{aligned} & L/(1 - T) & (2) \\ & = \$14,077/(1 - .4) \\ & = \$23,461 \end{aligned}$$

Stated differently, a reduction in the annual rental charge by $23,461 will reduce taxes by $9,384, so that the after-tax rental is reduced by $14,077.

To recap this section: If a lessor is able to use investment tax credits which would otherwise be lost to a prospective lessee, the benefits may be passed on, in whole or part, to the lessee as lower rental payments. The lessor must equate the present value of the reduction in rentals (after tax), with the amount of the investment credit. This measures the *maximum* rent reduction, although in practical cases the lease bargain would divide the benefit between lessor and lessee.

Rapid Write-off Depreciation Methods

Depreciation represents the decline in an asset's value over its useful life, and is a tax-deductible expense. In order to stimulate business investment in new plant and equipment, the Congress has permitted a variety of rapid write-off, or accelerated, depreciation methods to be used on business tax returns. Larger depreciation expenses in the early years of asset life entail a delay of tax payments until later years. The *present value* of a series of tax payments is lower if the tax payments are postponed, since the funds can be put to work in the interim. In other words, accelerated depreciation increases the economic value of a capital expenditure.

Similar to the case of investment tax credits, there are circumstances where companies are unable to take full advantage of fast write-offs of asset cost. For example, a company with a history of operating losses might be unable to realize benefits from accelerated depreciation, and might even attempt to postpone depreciation expenses lest the tax benefits be lost. Yet a prospective lessor might be able to use the tax benefits, and pass them on to the lessee in the form of lower rentals.

In order to illustrate this point, we will briefly review the depreciation methods described in Chapter 4 and then extend the example to show its effect on lease negotiations. Recall that most business assets are depreciated following one of three methods:

1. *Straight line depreciation (SL).* The cost of the asset, C, less salvage, S, is spread evenly over the asset's life of N years. Depreciation, D, is:

$$D = \frac{C - S}{N} \tag{3}$$

and the straight line *rate* is $1/N$.

2. *Double declining balance depreciation (DDB).* There is a family of declining balance depreciation methods, among which double declining balance offers the fastest write-off of asset cost. Each year's depreciation charge is computed by applying double the straight line rate, or $2/N$, to the asset's book value. Since book value is defined as cost less accumulated depreciation, each year's depreciation charge is computed on a smaller base. Each year's ending book value, BV_t, is given by the following expression:

$$BV_t = C(1 - 2/N)^t \tag{4}$$

and the depreciation charge in year t can be computed as

$$D_t = BV_t - BV_{t-1} \tag{5}$$

or

$$D_t = C([1 - 2/N]^t - [1 - 2/N]^{t-1})$$

In the earlier years of asset life, DDB depreciation will substantially exceed the SL amounts. Also, while the DDB calculation does not consider salvage value directly, the asset is never to be depreciated below estimated salvage value.

3. *Sum of years digits depreciation (SYD).* Each year's depreciation is a fraction which is applied to cost less salvage. The numerator is the number of years remaining in the asset's life, and the denominator is the sum of the digits in the useful life. A shortcut formula is:

$$D_t = \frac{(N-t+1)}{N(N+1)/2}(C-S) \tag{6}$$

For example, the first year's depreciation on a ten-year-lived asset would be:

$$D_1 = \frac{(10-1+1)}{10(10+1)/2}(C-S)$$

$$= \frac{10}{55}(C-S)$$

Chapter 4 applied each of these three depreciation methods to the case of an asset costing $100,000, lasting ten years with an estimated salvage value of $10,000. For a company taxed at 52 percent and with an after-tax cost of capital of 10 percent, the present value of the depreciation tax shields was found to be (from Chapter 4, page 00):

	Present Value of Depreciation Tax Deduction
SL method	$32,613.92
DDB method	$39,489.45
SYD method	$36,659.11

To show the possible impact of depreciation on lease negotiations, assume that a prospective lessee does not have sufficient taxable income to use rapid write-off depreciation. A lessor who is able to use DDB depreciation would increase the economic value of the asset by $6,875.53, computed as follows:

$39,489.45　present value of DDB depreciation
32,613.92　present value of SL depreciation
$ 6,875.53　difference, or increase in economic value available under a leasing arrangement

From this point, our analysis parallels our earlier reasoning for the investment credit. The fact that the tax shield is worth $6,875.53 more to the lessor than to the lessee can be translated into the maximum effect on the annual lease payment, as follows:

$$\begin{array}{ll}\text{Present value of difference} \\ \text{in tax shield using DDB}\end{array} = \begin{array}{l}\text{present value of after-tax} \\ \text{reduction in lease} \\ \text{payments}\end{array}$$

$$\$6,875.53 = L \times \sum_{t=1}^{N} 1/(1+K_{mc})^N \qquad (1)$$

For example, if the lease term is ten years and the lessor is taxed at 52 percent and the after-tax cost of capital is 12 percent, then

$$\$6,875.53 = L \times \sum_{t=1}^{10} 1/(1+.12)^t$$

$$\$6,875.33 = L \times 5.650$$

$$L = \$1,217$$

Since the after-tax effect on the lease payment has just been calculated as $1,217 and the tax rate is 52 percent, the effect on the *before*-tax lease payment is $2,335 ($1,217/[1-.52]). In other words, because the lessor is able to use DDB depreciation, the annual rental may be set $2,335 lower than if the lessor was required to use straight line depreciation.

Additional Aspects of Depreciation

While the above discussion presents the rudiments of depreciation calculations, there are a number of constraints and special features involved in their application. Among the more important are the following:

Eligible Property

The depreciation deduction is allowable only on property used in trade or business, or otherwise held for the production of income. Inventories and stock in trade are not depreciable.

Owner of Property

The owner of property suffers any economic loss from the decrease in property value, so only the owner is entitled to a depreciation deduction. Generally, property under lease is considered owned by the lessor, but in some cases the IRS may *interpret* a lease as a sale. This issue is discussed in some detail later in this chapter.

Changes in Depreciation Method

Usually a change in an adopted method of depreciation is a change in accounting method that requires IRS approval. But no IRS permission is required to change from declining balance to the straight line method. Often the present value of the depreciation tax shield can be increased by such a switch in depreciation method. The best time to switch depends upon the property life, salvage value, and cost of capital.

ADR System

In 1971 the IRS established the Class Life Asset Depreciation Range (ADR) system, which allows taxpayers to choose
from a range of depreciation lives that are not more than 20
percent below or above IRS guideline lives. Practically, the
ADR system allows assets to be depreciated over a shorter
"useful" life, thereby increasing the value of the depreciation
tax shield. In addition, the ADR system allows taxpayers to
disregard salvage value entirely in calculating depreciation,
except that assets are not to be depreciated *below* estimated
salvage values.

Lease v. Sale: A Question of Ownership

A fundamental question in the leasing area involves
distinguishing between a true lease and a conditional sale.
Very important tax consequences follow from this distinction.
For example, if a purported lease is interpreted by the IRS as a
sale, the lessor is affected as follows: (1) rental receipts are reinterpreted as installment payments of the purchase price,
with some portion of each payment being reinterpreted as interest on the installment debt; (2) any gain on the sale will
usually be treated as ordinary income, which is not eligible for
lower capital gains tax rates; and (c) the lessor will not be eligible for the investment tax credit.

Similar tax consequences affect the lessee: rental payments are reinterpreted as installment debt payments, so that
only the imputed interest on these payments is a tax-deductible expense; and if the property has been used previously by
the lessor, the amount of investment tax credit will be limited
and the choice of depreciation method will be restricted.

Given these radically different tax consequences of interpreting a transaction as a lease or a sale, it is wise to be alert
to the standards that have been used by the IRS in making this
distinction. Generally, if the lessee has the right to use the
leased property over its entire useful life, this is the equivalent

of ownership. The IRS has provided guidelines which state that any of the following conditions would warrant interpreting a lease agreement as a sale for tax purposes:

1. Portions of the rentals specifically apply to the building of an equity in the property by the lessee.
2. The lessee will acquire title to the property after paying the contractual rentals.
3. Lease payments over a relatively small portion of the property's total useful life constitute a large portion of the amount which the lessee would pay to obtain title.
4. Rental payments materially exceed the property's fair rental value.
5. The lease includes a purchase option at a nominal price which is expected to be well below market price, and which is small compared with the total rental payments.
6. Some portion of the rental payments is specifically designated as interest.

Guidelines containing phrases such as "relatively small," "materially," "fair," and so on require careful interpretation, and generally the tax courts rely upon *sets* of circumstances, especially those revealing the *intentions* of both parties to the lease. Usually the tax courts view the option or renewal price as a very significant factor in deciding whether a transaction is a true lease or a purchase. If an option price or renewal rent is clearly below the expected fair market value when the option may be exercised, this implies that earlier rentals are intended by the lessee to build an equity in the property. On the other hand, if the lessee has use of the property for a period which is short relative to the property's economic life and then must return the property to the lessor without any bargain renewal or purchase option, there is clearly a lease. Most practical cases fall between these extremes and require careful documentation of the intentions of lessor and lessee.

Sale and Leaseback

A difficult area in deciding whether a true lease exists concerns a sale and leaseback transaction. In such arrangements the owner of the property sells the property to a lessor, and the sales agreement requires that the property be leased back to the seller. Generally, the IRS acknowledges that sales and leasebacks are an accepted and useful way of controlling business property. However, it may be necessary to prove that the alleged owner of the property, the lessor, has indeed purchased a significant ownership interest in the property. The owner of property is one who is exposed to the usual risks and rewards of ownership.

The basic distinction between debtor/creditor bargains and purchaser/seller bargains must guide the interpretation of a sale and leaseback transaction. Between debtors and creditors it is agreed that the funds currently being paid to the debtor will be repaid with interest over a fixed future period. On the other hand, between sellers and purchasers it is agreed that the seller conveys property to the buyer, who then bears the usual risks of ownership. For example, if a purported sale and leaseback arrangement insures that the lessor will receive no more nor less than a return of investment plus a fixed interest charge, the IRS will interpret this as a debtor/creditor bargain and not a sale and leaseback.

Leveraged Leases as Tax Shelter Devices

In recent years tax law features such as accelerated depreciation, investment credits, and the shortening of useful lives under the ADR system have greatly diminished the importance of leasing as a means for the *lessee* to use leases as a means of accelerating tax deductions. This decline has been matched by an increasing emphasis on the use of leases as a tax shelter by *lessors*, and especially in the growth of *leveraged lease* arrangements. The basic features of leveraged leases, together with forms for the financial evaluation of leveraged lease arrangements, are presented in Chapter 8. The typical features are these:

1. A limited partnership is formed, with the primary goal of sheltering investors' income from other (non-leasing) sources; one partner serves as promoter.

2. The promoter locates a prospective lessee of business machinery or equipment and also contacts a prospective lender, such as a bank or insurance company.

3. The partnership purchases the property to be leased, financing the purchase with a 20 to 30 percent down payment and borrowing the remainder. The debt financing is on a nonrecourse basis, so that the lender's security for the loan is limited to the value of the equipment.

4. The partnership leases the equipment to the lessee at a rental sufficient to repay the loan and generate a modest before-tax profit.

5. The partnership elects the depreciation method providing the largest tax benefits in early years. Usually the partnership will manage to report substantial tax losses during the first several years of the lease.

In order to obtain the desired result in sheltering lessor taxes on other income, the lessor must be the *owner* of the property for tax purposes. Since the lessor's tax savings arise from (1) the return of much of the lessor's equity investment almost immediately, in the form of an investment tax credit, and (2) the lessor's use of tax losses provided in the early part of the lease term, mainly from depreciation and other deductions, the ownership issue is critical.

The increasing prominence of *leveraged leasing* and the wide variety of leveraged lease arrangements have led the IRS to promulgate a special set of leveraged lease guidelines, directed toward assuring that the lessor is indeed the tax owner of the leased property. The main issues covered by the guidelines are (1) the lessor's equity, (2) lessee's investment, (3) residual value, (4) purchase option, (5) profitability, and (6) cash flow. Each of these issues deserves some attention:

1.   *Lessor's equity.* The lessor's equity must be at least 20 percent of the total cost of the property at the start of the lease, and must *remain* at this level over the lease term.

To show how the minimum investment is maintained, we must first define:

A = Cumulative payments by the lessee (mainly the rental payments to the lessor)

B = Cumulative payments by the lessor (primarily debt service)

C = Excess lessor investment (lessor down payment in excess of 20% of property's cost)

D = Prorata share of profits (total profits are usually assumed to be earned evenly over the lease term; in some cases uneven rental payments of varying interest expenses will justify departing from this assumption)

The rule for maintaining minimum investment is this: at no point during the lease term may A − B exceed C + D. In other words, the excess of lessor cash receipts over cash disbursements (A − B) is limited to a recovery of any excess investment plus a pro rata share of profits (C + D).

As an illustration of compliance with this test, assume that property with a total cost of $125,000 is to be leased at an annual rate of $18,000, and at the end of the lease term the residual value is expected to be $30,000. Financing is 20 percent equity ($25,000) and 80 percent debt ($100,000). The cost of borrowing is 12 percent per annum, and the debt will be repaid in ten equal annual installments of $17,700 (including principal and interest).

The lessor's initial equity of 20 percent equals the IRS minimum requirement, as there is no "excess" investment in this example. Total depreciation expense is $95,000 ($125,000 cost less $30,000 salvage), and interest expense is $77,000 (repayments of $177,000, and $100,000 borrowed). Total profit is $8,000 (total rentals of $180,000, less depreciation of $95,000 and interest of $77,000).

The following table shows a year-by-year calculation of the maximum amount which can be recovered by the lessor each year while meeting the investment maintenance test:

(All figures in thousands of dollars)

Year	A. Cumula-tive Rents	B. Cumula-tive Debt Service	C. Excess Investment	D. Pro Rata Profit	Test (A-B) - (C + D)
1	18	17.7	0	.8	1.1
2	36	35.4	0	1.6	2.2
3	54	53.1	0	2.4	3.3
4	72	70.8	0	3.2	4.4
5	90	85.5	0	4.0	5.5
6	108	106.2	0	4.8	6.6
7	126	123.9	0	5.6	7.7
8	144	141.6	0	6.4	8.8
9	162	159.3	0	7.2	9.9
10	180	177.0	0	8.0	11.0

The compliance test is met in this example, since the numbers in the final column do not go below zero during the lease term. Notice that the calculations are carried through on a *before*-tax basis, as is required by the IRS for the purposes of this test. Since the tax consequences such as investment tax credits and rapid depreciation write-offs have important additional effects on lessor cash flows, it is quite likely that many otherwise economically desirable leases will fail to meet the profit test shown above. Recently Congress extended the leveraged lease rules to require that the lessor's losses from the leveraged lease, which can be used to offset positive income from other operations, be limited to the amount of investment that the lessor has "at risk" in any given year.

2. *Lessee's investment.* No member of the lessee group may invest in any part of the leased property. This also prohibits either lending by the lessee to the lessor or lessee guarantees of indebtedness of the lessor, if such transactions are related to acquiring the property to be leased.

There are two elements in this requirement: (1) lessee investment in the original cost of the property, and (2) leasehold improvements by the lessee. Essentially, the fact that a lessee makes substantial leasehold improvements (which are often described as extraordinary maintenance and repairs) may increase the market value of the property for the lessor. In such cases the IRS may argue that the lessee's expenditures were a disguised form of participation in the property cost.

3. *Residual value*. The residual value of the property must be substantial, equal to at least 20 percent of original cost; and it must be expected that at lease termination the property will have a remaining period of use equal to at least 20 percent of its original estimated life. Thus the residual value must *not* be solely value as scrap, but must reflect continuing business use of the property.

This portion of the IRS guidelines also includes the curious requirement that the estimate of residual value must be determined *without* regard to general inflation. Yet there is no clear method provided to remove the effect of inflation from other courses of change in value; this difficult issue awaits clarification, perhaps by the tax courts. One plausible (though untested) interpretation is that 20 percent of the *purchasing power* invested in the property must be expected to be received at the end of the lease as residual value. For example, under this interpretation a property costing $100,000 and leased for ten years when the expected inflation rate is 9 percent would require a residual value of $47,347, computed as follows:

$100,000	cost of property today
2.367	inflation factor: the compound interest factor at 9% for 10 years is 2.367, obtained by using the *reciprocal* of the present value factor for 10 years at 9% (Table A-2), i.e., 1/.3855 = 2.367
———	
236,700	
× .20	residual value percentage requirement
$ 47,347	residual value requirement, in dollars 10 years hence

4. *Purchase option*. The lessee must not have a right to either purchase or re-lease the property at the end of the lease term *except* at the fair market value of the property or the fair rental value, to be determined at that date.

5. *Profitability*. Lessor must be able to show that the lease is profitable *without* regard to tax effects. This means

that the rents plus residual values should exceed the debt service plus the equity investment. On the surface, this curious requirement inherently subverts the basic intent of the Congress in providing investment tax credits and rapid depreciation methods to stimulate business investment. These tax incentives to investment reflect a presumption by economic policy makers that many business capital expenditures would appear unacceptable, except for favorable income tax consequences. On the other hand, the IRS has often stated a position that business transactions should not be motivated *solely* by tax consequences, i.e., that there should exist a sound business rationale apart from anticipated tax benefits. It is difficult to reconcile the views of economic policy makers and the stated position of the IRS on the role of tax consequences in motivating business investment. For the present, in designing leveraged lease arrangements it is important to comply with the profit restriction imposed by the IRS guidelines.

6. *Cash flow requirement.* The lessor is constrained to receive a substantial cash flow from the lease, so that the total rent exceeds the total debt service by at least 2 to 4 percent of the investment times the number of years in the lease. It is important to distinguish between cash flow and profit: a profitable project may fail to generate a positive cash flow, and conversely a project with an adequate cash flow may be unprofitable. This is so since the cash flow definition used by the IRS *excludes* the initial cost of the property and its residual value at the end of the lease term. Applying this rule to our earlier example:

$180,000	total rent (10 years at $18,000)
177,000	debt service (10 years at 17,700)
$ 3,000	net cash flow
Standard:	equity investment × 10 years × 2%
	= $25,000 × 10 × .02
	= $5,000

So in this case we find that the cash flow amount fails to meet the standard.

Summary

A variety of tax incentives to business investment can be used more effectively through leasing arrangements. *Whenever potential lessees and lessors are taxed at different rates, or differ in their abilities to use rapid write-off depreciation methods or investment tax credits, then the potential may exist for a mutually profitable lease arrangement.*

Initially, the tax analysis of leases focused on the lessee's perspective, since rentals were often used as a method of accelerating tax deductions for the cost of using leased assets. Such motives became less important with the advent of investment credits, more accelerated methods of tax depreciation, and the ADR system for setting useful lives. The focus has recently shifted to the lessor's tax position, and a variety of leveraged lease arrangements have become popular. In order to assure that such arrangements have a business purpose other than tax consequences, the IRS has promulgated a set of leveraged lease guidelines, which were discussed in this chapter.

While this chapter's discussion should serve to alert the businessperson to the broad tax consequences and constraints in lease negotiation, *it is imperative to recognize that tax law is a highly specialized field of professional practice with a continually changing body of legislation, rulings, and court cases.* An attempt to encapsulate relevant features of this body of knowledge in a short and readable discussion almost inevitably introduces overgeneralizations. Here again *you are urged to seek the advise of a competent tax specialist before you approach the table to design lease arrangements.* However, our discussion should have the merit of alerting you to the questions to ask.

CHAPTER 6

Analysis of Lease Profitability after Taxes: Lessor's Perspective

Little attention is paid in business publications to the lessor's problems in determining the rental he will need to negotiate with the lessee. In fact, in some respects, he has the more complicated set of issues to tackle. In this chapter the lessor negotiates a simple lease, i.e., one in which the lessor will not explicitly rely on creditors to assist in financing his ownership of the asset. Termed a nonleveraged lease, the transaction involves two parties, the lessor and lessee. We do not have to consider the effect of the lessor's creditors (if any) on the terms of the deal. Chapter 8, on the other hand, treats leveraged leasing, which explicitly takes account of third-party creditors financing the asset to be placed on lease by the lessor.

This chapter addresses only one question, What rental should the lessor charge for the use of the asset?

Capital Budgeting Decision

Whether from the perspective of the lessor or lessee, leasing represents a capital budgeting decision. Capital budgeting focuses on projects (in our case a lease) and analyzes the profitability of a project based upon the *incremental* cash inflows and outflows which are traceable to the existence of the project (or lease) and which would disappear if the project were dropped.

To illustrate, suppose a lessor had negotiated a lease for five years with a net rental income (after tax) of $37,000 ($A_t$); the cost of the leased asset (C) came to $100,000; the investment tax credit (ITC) amounted to $10,000 receivable at the end of the first year. His cost of financing (K_{mc}) equals 10 percent after tax. All cash flows are payable at the end of the indicated years. What is the NPV of the lease?

Cash Inflows:
    $37,000 (5 years @ .10) × 3.791* = $140,267
      10,000 (1 year @ .10) ×   .909* =   9,090
    Total inflows $149,357

    Less

Cash Outflows:
    Investment   100,000
NPV $ 49,357

*Interest factors from Appendix Tables A-1 and A-2, respectively. The format above is an application of Expression 1 in Chapter 3.

The results of this net present value calculation mean the investor (lessor) (a) will recover his investment ($100,000), (b) will earn 10 percent on that investment, and (c) has an excess value of $49,357.

The internal rate of return (IRR), *that rate of return which would reduce the NPV to zero*, is also derived from the NPV formula discussed in Chapter 3:

$$NPV = A_t \times \sum_{t=1}^{N} \frac{1}{(1+R)} - I \qquad (1)$$

when A_t represents the cash inflow for each period. Using the information for the present case, where the investment credit of $10,000 is received at the end of the first year, and an amount of five rentals of $37,000 will be received at the end of each year:

$$NPV = \$37,000 \times \sum_{t=1}^{5} \frac{1}{(1+R)^t} + \frac{\$10,000}{(1+R)} - \$100,000 = 0 \quad (2)$$

R, the internal rate of return, is found by a process of trial and error. Let's try 28 percent and 30 percent from Table 1 in the Appendix.

At 28 percent, NPV is found thus:

$37,000 × 2.532 =	$ 93,684
10,000 × .781 =	7,810
Present value of cash inflows	$101,494

At 30 percent, NPV is found thus:

$37,000 × 2.436 =	$90,132
10,000 × .769 =	7,690
Present value of cash inflows	$98,822

To find the approximate IRR, we interpolate between 28 percent and 30 percent:

28% =	$101,494
X =	100,000 or NPV = 0
30% =	98,822
2% =	$ 2,672

$$\frac{1,494}{2.672} = .56$$

Then IRR = 28% + .56 = 28.56%.

Since the proposed lease has a positive NPV ($49,357; and/or an IRR $> K_{mc}$ (28.56% $>$ 10%), the lessor would look on the project favorably.

Applying the Lessor's Rule

The above concepts all bear on the lessor's decision about the level at which to fix rentals. To obtain the rental he will apply the following decision rule: *namely, to set a rental such that the present value of the rental cash inflows* (R_t) *will equal or exceed the cost of the asset* (C) *less the present value of the tax credit* (PV_{ITC}) *less the present value of the salvage* (PV_S) *less the present value of the depreciation tax shield* (PV_{DT}) *plus the present value of the operating expenses* (PV_O) *associated with the lease*. The expression becomes:

$$C - PV_{ITC} - PV_S - PV_{DT} + PV_O = R_t \times \sum_{t=1}^{N} \frac{1}{(1 + K_{mc})^t} \qquad (3)$$

We must now solve for R_t.

Assume a lease proposal with the following terms:

Lease term (N)	8 years
Asset life	10 years
Asset cost (C)	$1,000,000
Residual value (S)	$200,000 (estimated at end of lease)
Investment tax credit (ITC)	$100,000 (received at end of first period)
Lessor's tax rate (T)	50%
Lessor's cost of capital (K_{mc})	15% (after tax)
Discount on salvage (K_S)	20% (after tax)
Operating expenses (O)	$1,000 (paid at end of each period)
Depreciation method:	Straight line

What rentals should be charged if:

1. Rents are paid at end of period?
2. Rents are paid at beginning of period?

Step 1—Present Value of Investment Tax Credit

$$PV_{ITC} = ITC \times \frac{1}{(1 + K_{mc})^t} = \$100,000 \times \frac{1}{(1 + .15)^1} \qquad (4)$$

From Table A-2 in the Appendix, the expression $\frac{1}{(1 = .15)^1}$ equals .86957, or, rounding, .870. Therefore

$$
\begin{aligned}
PV_{ITC} &= ITC \times IF \\
&= \$100,000 \times .870 \\
&= \$87,000
\end{aligned}
$$

Step 2—Present Value of Salvage or Residual

$$PV_S = S \times \frac{S}{(1 + K_S)^N} = \$200,000 \times \frac{1}{(1 + .20)^8} \qquad (5)$$

From Table A-2 in the Appendix, the expression $\frac{1}{(1 + .20)^8}$ gives an IF of .23257, or, rounding, .232. Therefore

$$
\begin{aligned}
PV_S &= S \times IF \\
&= \$200,000 \times .233 \\
&= \$46,600
\end{aligned}
$$

Step 3—Present Value of Operating Expenses after Tax

$$PV_O = O(1 - T) \times \sum_{t=1}^{8} \frac{1}{(1 + K_{mc})^t} \qquad (6)$$

$$= 1,000(1 - .50) \times \sum_{t=1}^{8} \frac{1}{(1 + .15)^t}$$

The interest factor (IF) from Table A-1 in the Appendix is 4.487 (rounded). Therefore

$$PV_o = O(1 - T) \times IF$$
$$= 1,000(1 - .50) \times 4.489$$
$$= \$2,244$$

Step 4—Present Value of the Depreciation Tax Savings

Remember that the depreciation tax savings (DT) are a benefit of ownership lost to the lessee. In our illustration, the firm uses the straight line method (Chapter 3). Accordingly, the amount to be depreciated is calculated:

Cost of asset	\$1,000,000	
Less		
Salvage	0	(Asset Depreciation over Ten Years)
Depreciable Cost	\$1,000,000	

$$\text{Annual depreciation} = \frac{\$1,000,000}{10} = \$100,000$$

Present value of depreciation tax savings is shown as (PV_{DT}).

$$PV_{DT} = (DT) \times \sum_{t=1}^{N} \frac{1}{(1 + K_{mc})^t} \qquad (7)$$

$$= \$100,000(.50) \times \sum_{t=1}^{10} \frac{1}{(1 + .15)^t}$$

The interest factor (IF) from Table A-1 in the Appendix is 5.019 (rounded) for 10 years at 15 percent. Hence

$$PV_{DT} = (DT) \times IF$$
$$= \$50,000 \times 5.019$$
$$= \$250,950$$

Step 5—What Should the Pretax Rent Be If Rentals Are Paid at the End of the Period (t)?

$$C - PV_{ITC} - PV_S - PV_{DT} + PV_O = R_t \times \sum_{t=1}^{N} \frac{1}{(1 + K_{mc})^t} \qquad (3)$$

$1,000,000 - \$87,000 - \$46,600$

$$- \$250,950 + \$2,244 = R \times \sum_{t=1}^{8} \frac{1}{(1 + .15)^t}$$

Then

$$\$617,694 = R_t \times \sum_{t=1}^{8} \frac{1}{(1 + .15)^t}$$

From the same table used in Step 4, the interest factor is 4.487 (rounded). Therefore

$$C - PV_{ITC} - PV_S - PV_{DT} + PV_O = R \times IF$$

and

$$\$617,694 = R \times 4.487$$

$$\$137,663 = R$$

The rental obtained represents the *after-tax rental*. The *pretax rental* charged the lessee is secured by:

$$\frac{R(\text{after tax})}{(1 - T)}$$

or

$$\frac{\$137,663}{(1 - .50)} = \$275,326 \text{ pre-tax rental}$$

Step 6—What Should Be the Pretax Rent If Rentals Are Paid at the Beginning of the Period (t)?

This case assumes that all cash flows *except salvage and depreciation tax savings* are payable at the beginning of each period. Expression (3) is revised to take account of the new time sequence:

$$C - ITC - PV_S - PV_{DT} + PV_O = R\left[1.0 + \sum_{t=1}^{N-1} \frac{1}{(1 + K_{mc})^t}\right] \quad (3)$$

The right-hand side of this expression reflects the fact that the first rental payment is received immediately and has no discount penalty (this is shown by the 1.0 inside the parentheses). In addition, there are $(N-1)$ equal periodic payments, ending on the *first* day of the last period, i.e., at time $(N-1)$, so the second term inside the parentheses is the interest factor for an ordinary annuity of $N-1$ payments.

Step 6A—Present Value of Operating Expenses

$$PV_O = O(1 - T)\left[1.0 + \sum_{t=1}^{N-1} \frac{1}{(1 + K_{mc})^t}\right]$$

$$= \$1000(1 - .50)\left[1.0 + \sum_{t=1}^{7} \frac{1}{(1 + .15)^t}\right]$$

$$= \$500[1.0 + IF^*]$$

$$= \$500[1.0 + 4.160]$$

$$= \$2,580$$

Step 6B—Solving for the Pretax Rental Charge

Using the revised Expression (3),

$$C - ITC - PV_S - PV_{DT} + PV_O = R\left[1.0 + \sum_{t=1}^{N-1} \frac{1}{(1 + K_{mc})^t}\right]$$

*From Table A-1 in the Appendix.

Then

$$\$1,000,000 - \$100,000 - \$46,600$$
$$- \$250,950 + \$2,244 = R\left[1 + \sum_{t=1}^{7} \frac{1}{(1+.15)^t}\right]$$

and

$$\$604,694 = R\left[1 + \sum_{t=1}^{7} \frac{1}{(1+.15)^t}\right]$$

From Appendix Table A-1, the expression $\sum_{t=1}^{7} \frac{1}{(1+.15)^t}$ yields an interest factor of 4.160 (rounded). Therefore

$$C - ITC - PV_S - PV_{DT} + PV_O = R[1.0 + IF]$$

and

$$\$604,694 = R[1.0 + 4.160]$$

$$\$117,189 = R \text{ (the after-tax rental)}$$

The Pretax Rental equals:

$$\frac{R(\text{after-tax rental})}{(1-T)} = \frac{\$117,189}{(1-.50)} =$$

$$\$234,378 \text{ pretax rental charged the lessee}$$

Sell or Lease

The preceding situation illustrates how a buyer *who has purchased equipment from the manufacturer may go about fixing a minimum rental on the equipment* on a subsequent lease. But what of the manufacturer who has the option to sell the equipment or lease the equipment? There are significant differences in his position. IBM, for example, may sell its computers or lease them. Savin Business Machines Corporation changed from a policy stressing sales to one that encourages leasing by offering longer lease plans and discounts from the usual rental without altering the sales price. Xerox Corporation took an opposite tack. Xerox shifted emphasis to sales with increased trade allowances, cut selling prices, and lowered the cost of full service maintenance agreements.

The differences between the lessee-buyer's decision to own or lease and the lessor-manufacturer's to sell or lease are mainly tax related. Moreover, the differences are noncomplementary; that is, the lessee's decision to buy or lease is not the other side of the lessor-manufacturer's coin to sell or lease. These differences include the following:

1. *Depreciation basis.* A manufacturer who elects to lease rather than sell includes only the manufacturing cost as his depreciation basis (Chapter 3). The anticipated profit on the sale of the asset cannot be part of the depreciable base. By contrast, a lessee-purchaser capitalizes the manufacturer's profit on the purchase price plus installation as his actual cost. This difference in the depreciation base can result in a substantive variation between lease v. buy for the lessee-purchaser and lease v. sell for the lessor-manufacturer. The two decisions are not symmetrical.

2. *Investment tax credit.* The investment tax credit equals 10 percent if the asset is held for seven years. The lessor-manufacturer may apply this rate against the manufacturing cost only. The lessee-purchaser, on the other hand, may apply the tax against the manufacturing cost plus the manufacturer's profit. The lessor-manufacturer enjoys a higher investment tax credit.

3. *Gain or loss sale of asset.* If the equipment is sold above book value before its economic life is terminated, the excess is taxable as ordinary income. Since the depreciation basis differs between the lessee-purchaser and the lessor-manufacturer, it follows that their tax obligations also differ.

Sell v. Lease Approach[1]

The analysis of the lessor-manufacturer's position rests upon several assumptions:

1. The manufacturer-lessor is indifferent to selling or leasing an asset as long as the net present value of the receipts under either alternative is the same. *The objective here is to determine the indifference point between sell and lease for the manufacturer.*

2. Differences in operating income or costs emanate solely from differences in the manner in which the asset is held. Thus if the lease requires the lessor to maintain the equipment, the rental incorporates the cost of the service.

3. Sales revenue or operational savings derived from the asset are going to be the same whether the asset is leased or purchased.

Step 1—Net Present Value of Outright Sale

The net present value of an outright sale will be the net selling price (S) *less the cost of producing the asset* (C) *times 1 minus the firm's marginal income tax rate* $(1 - T)$. The expression becomes:

$$NPV = \frac{(S - C)(1 - T)}{(1 + K_{mc})}$$
$$= \frac{(\$300,000 - \$150,000)(1 - .48)}{(1 + .10)} = \frac{\$78,000}{(1.10)} \qquad (8)$$

where the manufacturer's cost is $150,000; his selling price, $300,000; his tax rate, 48 percent; and after-tax cost of capital (K_{mc}), 10 percent. The NPV of outright sale with payments at the end of the period would equal:

$$NPV \text{ of outright sale} = \frac{\$78,000}{(1.10)}$$

Using Table A-2 in the Appendix, the expression $\frac{1}{1.10}$ equals .909 (rounded), and $\$78,000 \times .909 = \$70,902$.

Step 2—Net Present Value of Cost of Leasing (Asset Cost)

Assume now the manufacturer has the additional data before him:

Cost of producing the asset (C)	$150,000
Investment tax credit (ITC) (payable at end of year 1)	10%
Depreciation: straight line[2] (no salvage)	$18,750
Firm's cost of capital (K_{mc})	10%
Firm's cost of new debt (K_D)	5%
Selling price of the asset (S)	$300,000
Book value of asset at end of lease (B)	0
Salvage (S_V)	0
Length of lease (and depreciable life of asset)	8 years
Annual lease rental (L_t)	to be determined
Tax rate (T)	.48
Payments made at end of each period (t)	

In general, the NPV of the leasing cost will equal the cost outflow of the asset to the manufacturer plus the present value investment tax credit plus the present value of the depreciation tax savings plus the present value of the after-tax salvage value. The formula becomes:

$$\text{NPV of lease cost} = -C + \frac{ITC}{(1+K_D)} + \sum_{t=1}^{N} \frac{D_t T}{(1+K_D)^t} + \frac{(S-B)(1-T)}{(1+K_{mc})^N} \quad (9)$$

Then, inserting the data,

$$\text{NPV of lease cost} = -\$150,000 + \frac{15,000}{1+.05} + \sum_{t=1}^{8} \frac{18,750(.48)}{(1.05)^t} + O*$$

Note that the cost of the asset constitutes an outlay and is a negative value ($-$ C). Reducing the figures:

$$\text{NPV of lease cost} = -150,000 + 14,286 + 58,167$$

$$= -\$77,547$$

Tables A-1 and A-2 in the Appendix are used to discount value of depreciation tax savings and cash savings from investment tax credit by our now familiar process. Table figures are rounded to three digits.

Step 3—Solving the Annual Rental for Lessor-Manufacturer

The lease rental such that the NPV of an outright sale equals the NPV of the lease alternative is computed as follows:

$$\text{NPV of outright sale} = \text{NPV of lease cost} + \text{NPV} \qquad (10)$$

of the annual rentals, where NPV of rentals $= L(1-T)\sum_{t=1}^{N} \frac{1}{(1+K_D)^t}$

Then, using Appendix Tables A-1 and A-2,

$$\$70,902 = -\$77,547 + L(1-T)\sum_{t=1}^{8} \frac{1}{(1.05)^t}$$

$$\$70,902 = -\$77,547 + L(.52)(6.463) =$$

$$\$70,902 = -\$77,547 + 3.360L$$

*Thus, there is no salvage or book value.

Transposing,

$$\$70,902 + 77,547 = 3.360L$$

$$\$148,449 = 3.360L$$

$$\$44,181 = L(\text{annual rental})$$

The value of L ($44,181) indicates that the NPV of the cash flows from selling the asset for $300,000 equals the NPV of the cash flows generated by leasing if the annual rental is $44,181. With this information, a manufacturer may be able to influence his sales/lease mix to achieve particular financial objectives. If the manufacturer wishes to encourage leasing and receive a lease rental of $44,181, he can increase the sales price of the asset. Alternatively, he could reduce the rental below $44,181 and make leasing the more favorable option for the lessee. In short, if the manufacturer knows his indifference point between selling the asset at $300,000 and renting it at $44,181 on an eight-year lease, he can move to induce leasing or purchasing by his customer.

Summary

In our illustrations the calculations give at least a minimum pretax rental below which the lessor should not go in negotiating the lease arrangement. If he goes below this minimum, he will not earn enough to maintain the value of the firm's securities and/or he will not recapture the cost of his equipment. Accordingly, he must decide the minimum return he will seek on the transaction and bargain upward from there.

The calculations may seem tedious, but they all involve a common procedure used whenever we borrow from our bank, namely, discounting. We are always estimating the present worth of money to be received (or paid) at some time in the future. If the problem is approached step by step, using the tables in the Appendix, the calculations are made expeditiously using a pocket calculator. The tables give us an interest factor (or discount factor) for a given interest rate covering a given period of time.

We used, in our illustrations, a time period of one year. This need not be the case. In practice, rentals are calculated on a monthly basis. The variation does not change the basic calculations except to increase the time period by a factor of 12. For example, an eight-year lease would require ninety-six time periods (N = 96) at the chosen discount rate. The tables in the Appendix allow for twenty time periods.

Finally, this chapter provides a useful background for the reasoning involved in leveraged leasing arrangements, which are discussed in Chapter 8.

CHAPTER 7

Analysis of Lease Profitability after Taxes: Lessee's Perspective

To the lessee, the lease decision presents itself as a decision between two alternatives, to lease or to own. In turn, questions of financing ownership arise which affect the analysis. There is also the problem of whether the asset acquisition is mandatory or discretionary. A mandatory investment is investment in an asset which must be obtained if the company chooses to remain in business. For example, the telephone company must provide the equipment to service all parts of its franchise area, even those segments that lose money; or environmental protection equipment may have to be installed or a particular operation abandoned. These considerations alter the analysis and give rise to three approaches to the analysis of the lessee's position. The selection of any single methodology depends on the circumstances of the lease agreement.

Cost Minimization Approach

This methodology assumes the following prevalent conditions:

1. The company has already decided to acquire the asset; either the investment is mandatory or its profitability is already established.

89

2. The company has decided to finance the acquisition, if owned, by debt *or treats* the lease as a form of debt.

3. The company can acquire the asset at the same cost as the lessor, and the amount of the loan equals the cost of equipment.

4. The question remaining, therefore, is simply, What is the least-cost method of financing the asset — borrow and buy or lease?

Let's assume the lessee has the following facts before him in making his decision on whether to lease or borrow and buy:

Rent Paid at End of Period

Cost of Equipment (C)	$200,000
Salvage value (S)	$6,667
Rental, if paid at end of period (L)	$78,866
Depreciation method(D)	sum of digits (SYD)
Operating costs of ownership (O)	$10,000
Term of lease and term of loan	10 years
Bank loan (P)	$200,000
Firm's weighted average cost of capital (K_{mc})	10% after tax
Discount factor applied to salvage (K_s)	20% after tax
Cost of new debt (K_d)	6% before tax
Ordinary corporate tax rate (T)	50%

Step 1—Annual Repayments (Amortization) of Bank Loan (B)

The principal of the loan (P) equals cost of equipment (C). The loan repayment (B) is found by:

$$P = B_t \times \sum_{t=1}^{N} \frac{1}{(1 + K_d)^t} \tag{1}$$

From table A-1 in the Appendix, the expression $\sum_{t=1}^{10} \frac{1}{(1 + .06)^t}$ reads as 6 percent for ten years, or 7.360. Therefore the short-cut formula reads:

$$P = B_t \times \text{interest factor}$$

$$\$200,000 = B_t \times 7.360$$

$$\$200,000 = 7,360 \, B_t$$

$$\$27,174 = B_t$$

On a \$200,000 loan, therefore, the lessee will pay \$27,174 for ten years. This sum includes interest and amortization of principal. The following schedule gives the breakdown between interest and principal. This breakdown is important because interest is tax deductible.

Year	Payment (B_t)	Interest (i)	Principal (P)	Balance
1	\$27,174	\$12,000	\$ 15,174	\$184,826
2	27,174	11,090	16,084	168,742
3	27,174	10,124	17,050	151,692
4	27,174	9,102	18,072	133,620
5	27,174	8,017	19,157	114,463
6	27,174	6,868	20,306	94,157
7	27,174	5,649	21,525	72,632
8	27,174	4,359	22,815	49,817
9	27,174	2,989	24,185	25,632
10	27,174	1,538	25,636	—
		\$71,736	\$200,000	

Step 2—Calculation of Depreciation (if asset is owned)

$$\text{Sum of years digits} = \frac{N(N + 1)}{2} \tag{2}$$

$$= \frac{10(10+1)}{2}$$

$$= \frac{110}{2}$$

$$= 55$$

Amount to Be Depreciated

Cost of asset	$200,000
Salvage	6,667
	$193,333

Again depreciation is a tax deduction belonging to the owner.

Year	SYD Factor	Depreciation*
1	10/55	$ 35,151
2	9/55	31,636
3	8/55	28,121
4	7/55	24,606
5	6/55	21,091
6	5/55	17,576
7	4/55	14,061
8	3/55	10,545
9	2/55	7,030
10	1/55	3,515
		$193,333

*Rounded to nearest dollar.

Step 3—Lease v. Borrow and Own Analysis—Decision Criterion

The cost of the borrow and buy alternative is the loan payments (B_t) *for each period* (t) *plus the operating expenses for each period* (O_t) *less the interest, depreciation, and operating expense tax savings* $([i + D + O] \times T)$ *less the after-tax residual values, if any, discounted at a rate appropriate to the risk of the cash flow* $(K_d$ *or* $K_s)$. In terms of a formula, this is expressed as:

$$\sum_{t=1}^{N} \frac{B_t + O_t - (i_t + D_t + O_t)T}{(1 + K_d[1 - T])^N} - \frac{S}{(1 + K_s)^N} \tag{3}$$

The cost of the lease alternative is the after-tax rental payments $(L_t[1-T])$ *for each period discounted by the after-tax cost of debt capital* $(K_d[1-T])$. The net for each period is summed to obtain the total. The formula expression is:

$$\sum_{t=1}^{N} \frac{L_t(1-T)}{(1+K_d[1-T])^N} \tag{4}$$

Expressions (3) and (4) put into a capsule the elements of the problem. However, they are easily converted to simple arithmetic:

(1) Year	(2) Loan Payment (B_t)	(3) Interest (i)	(4) Principal (P)	(5) Balance	(6) Deprecia-tion (D)
0					
1	$27,174	$12,000	$15,174	$184,826	$35,151
2	27,174	11,090	16,084	168,742	31,636
3	27,174	10,124	17,050	151,692	28,121
4	27,174	9,102	18,072	133,620	24,606
5	27,174	8,017	19,157	114,463	21,091
6	27,174	6,868	20,306	94,157	17,576
7	27,174	5,649	21,525	72,632	14,061
8	27,174	4,359	22,815	49,817	10,545
9	27,174	2,989	24,185	25,632	7,030
10	27,174	1,538	25,636	—	3,515

(7) Operating Costs	(8) $(8 = 3 + 6 + 7)$ Tax Deduction	(9) $(9 = 8 \times 50\%)$ Tax Savings	(10) $(10 = 1 + 7 - 9)$ Net Owner-ship Cost
$10,000	$57,151	$28,575	$ 8,599
10,000	52,726	26,363	10,811
10,000	48,245	24,122	13,052
10,000	43,708	21,854	15,320
10,000	39,108	19,554	17,620
10,000	34,444	17,222	19,952
10,000	29,710	14,855	22,319
10,000	24,904	12,452	24,722
10,000	20,019	10,010	27,164
10,000	15,053	7,526	29,648

(11)	(12) (12 = 11 − 10)	(13)	(14) (14 = 12 × 13)
After-Tax Rental	Advantage to Ownership	Discount Factor $(K_d = 6\% \times .50 = 3\%)$	Present Value to Own
39,433	$30,834	.971	$ 29,940
39,433	28,622	.943	26,991
39,433	26,381	.915	24,139
39,433	24,113	.888	21,412
39,433	21,813	.863	18,825
39,433	19,481	.837	16,306
39,433	17,114	.813	13,914
39,433	14,711	.789	11,607
39,433	12,269	.766	9,398
39,433	9,785	.744	7,280
	Salvage 6,667	.162	1,080
Present value advantage to Ownership			$180,892

Based on this analysis, the lessee should either reject the lease proposition or negotiate a lower rental based upon the tax savings available to him.

Rent Paid at Beginning of Period

Assume now that if rents are paid at beginning of period, the lessee will pay $71,689 per year.

(1) Year	(2) Loan Payment (B_t)	(3) Interest (i)	(4) Principal (P)	(5) Balance	(6) Depreciation
0					
1	$27,174	$12,000	$15,174	$184,826	$35,151
2	27,174	11,090	16,084	168,742	31,636
3	27,174	10,124	17,050	151,692	28,121
4	27,174	9,102	18,072	133,620	24,606
5	27,174	8,017	19,157	114,463	21,091
6	27,174	6,868	20,306	94,157	17,576
7	27,174	5,649	21,525	72,632	14,061
8	27,174	4,359	22,815	49,817	10,545
9	27,174	2,989	24,185	25,632	7,030
10	27,174	1,538	25,636	—	3,515

(7) Operating Costs	(8) (8 = 3 + 6 + 7) Tax Deduction	(9) (9 = 8 × 50%) Tax Savings	(10) (10 = 1 + 7 − 9 Net Owner-ship Cost
$10,000	$57,151	$28,575	$ 8,599
10,000	52,726	26,363	10,811
10,000	48,245	24,122	13,052
10,000	43,708	21,854	15,320
10,000	39,108	19,554	17,620
10,000	34,444	17,222	19,952
10,000	29,710	14,855	22,319
10,000	24,904	12,452	24,722
10,000	20,019	10,010	27,164
10,000	15,053	7,526	29,648

(11) After-Tax Rental	(12) (12 = 11 − 10) Advantage to Ownership	(13) Discount Factor $(K_d = 6\% \times .50 = 3\%)$	(14) (14 = 12 × 13) Present Value to Own
$35,844	$35,844	.000	$ 35,844
35,844	27,245	.971	26,455
35,844	25,033	.943	23,606
35,844	22,792	.915	20,856
35,844	20,524	.888	18,225
35,844	18,224	.863	15,727
35,844	15,892	.837	13,302
35,844	13,525	.813	10,996
35,844	11,122	.789	8,775
35,844	8,680	.766	6,649
—	(29,648)	.744	(22,058)
	Salvage 6,667	.162	1,080
Advantage to Ownership			$ 158,540

Note the following in the preceding situations:

1. Although the advantage is with ownership in both instances, the rents are lower if paid at the beginning of the period, and the advantage to ownership is also lower.

2. Both the ownership side of the equation and the lease side were discounted by the *after-tax cost of new debt*. This rate is taken to approximate the risk free rate of interest for the lessee company. Remember the analysis assumes the company has already decided to acquire the asset; that is, it has already evaluated the *profitability and risk* of the investment.

3.   The salvage value is not taxable. No profit was made (or anticipated) on the disposal of the asset. The firm simply planned to recover its book investment. The investment tax credit (not included in the two situations examined) would not have altered the tax status of the salvage figured on the gross investment cost but would have improved the cash flows of ownership, making it an even more attractive alternative.

4.   Other tax-deductible expenses of ownership could have been added to the borrow and buy side of the analysis. These would have decreased the advantage of ownership but would not have changed the format of the analysis. On the other hand, if such expenses were absorbed by the lessor and not fully passed on through higher rentals, leasing would become more attractive. The format is flexible for the addition or subtraction of expenses related to ownership or leasing.

5.   If a wholly cash purchase were made, the firm would lose the interest deduction and tax saving in filing with the IRS. But recall the discussion on cost of capital in Chapter 4: there is no free capital. If the firm drew the cost of the equipment from working capital, it would have to substitute another rate *for purpose of financial analysis*. This other rate might still be the cost of debt or what the money could earn if invested elsewhere or the firm's cost of capital. In any event, the firm would lose the interest tax savings on the lease v. buy project, thus making ownership less attractive. The same reasoning applies to a purchase combining a down payment in cash with the balance financed by a loan.

6.   Take care in arranging the variables for financial analysis. For example, if operating expenses are absorbed by the owner, do not add them to the cost of ownership and the cost of leasing. You cannot have it both ways. You may add expenses not absorbed by the lessor to either the cost of leasing *or* the cost of ownership — not both.

Figure 7-1 presents a schematic arrangement of the cash flows under the cost minimization approach.

Figure 7-1. Cash Flow Sequence: Cost Minimization
Analysis of Lease v. Buy

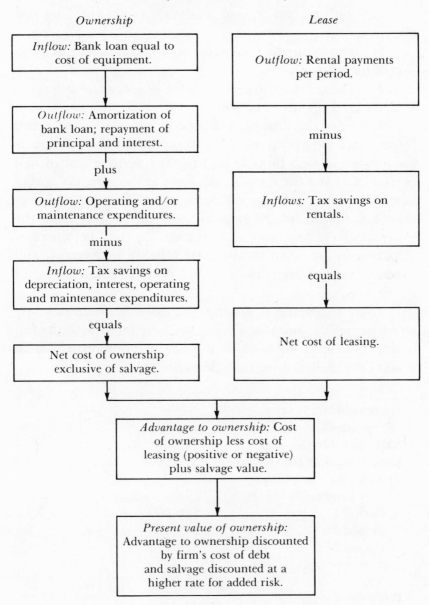

Lease Project Approach

This second type of analysis assumes the following circumstances:

1.   The company has made no decision on the acquisition of the asset.

2.   The company treats the lease as a separate *project* to be compared against ownership.

3.   Since the firm has made no prior analysis and treats leasing and ownership as two separate projects, it discounts the ownership cash flows at its weighted average cost of new capital (K_{mc}) and the leasing cash flows at the after-tax cost of new debt (K_d). The weighted average cost of new capital contains a premium for the risks of ownership arising from the *uncertainties* of operating expenses, etc. By contrast, the rental payments are fixed by the lease (certain in amount) and therefore no risk premium is included in the risk-free rate of the firm (K_d).

These differences in assumptions can lead to substantially different results. Suppose a company were faced with the following possibility to acquire a piece of equipment, which would have the following cash flow effects:

Increase annual sales revenues (A)	$50,000
Salvage value (S)	$4,000
Cost of equipment (C)	$120,000
*Depreciation, SYD (3-year project; N = 3)	
Period 1	$58,000
Period 2	$38,280
Period 3	$19,720
Annual operating costs (O)	$2,000
Ordinary corporate tax rate (T)	50%

*Normally, a lease of this term would not qualify for accelerated depreciation. We use this time frame only to illustrate the analysis.

Cost of capital (K) after
    tax   10%
Cost of new debt (K_d),
    after tax   3%
Discount factor applied to
    salvage value (after tax)   20%
Rent, if paid at end of
    period (L) $47,320

Net Present Value without Regard to Lease or Own

	Periods		
Tax Liability	*1*	*2*	*3*
Incremental sales (A)	$50,000	$50,000	$ 50,000
Operating expenses (O)	(2,000)	(2,000)	(2,000)
Depreciation	(58,000)	(38,280)	(19,720)
Taxable income	($10,000)	$ 9,720	$ 28,280
Tax at rate T (= 50%)	(5,000)	$ 4,860	$ 14,140
Net Operating Cash Flows			
Incremental sales (A)	$50,000	$50,000	$ 50,000
Operating expenses (O)	(2,000)	(2,000)	(2,000)
Tax liability or savings	5,000	(4,860)	(14,140)
Net operating cash flows	$53,000	$43,140	$33,860

Net Present Value (NPV)
Present value of operating cash flows (using Table A-2)

$53,000 × .909	$ 48,177
43,140 × .826	35,634
33,860 × .751	25,429
Total	$109,240
Present value of salvage	
$4,000 (3 years @ 20%) × .579	2,316
Total	$111,556
Less	
Cost of equipment	120,000
Net present value	($8,444)

Unlike the cost minimization approach (which assumes
the company has decided to acquire the project), the negative
NPV would cause rejection of the project and further analysis
would be halted. On the other hand, taking our second ap-

proach, further analysis looking at the lease as a separate project might suggest acquisition of the asset under different financial arrangements.

The second approach uses Net Present Value (NPV) as the decision criterion. The incremental sales revenues are excluded from the calculation as they affect ownership and leasing in the same way. *Therefore the net present value of ownership is the sum (Σ) of the depreciation tax shield ($T[D_t]$) less the after-tax operating costs ($O[1-T]$) for each period discounted at the firm's average cost of capital K_{mc}) plus the after-tax salvage value ($S[1-T]$) discounted at some higher rate K_s) less the cost of equipment (C).*

The net present value of leasing by comparison is the sum (Σ) of the after-tax rentals ($L[1-T]$) for each period discounted at the cost of debt (K_d) after tax. The total is added to the present value of ownership.

In shorthand, if P represents ownership and L, leasing,

$$\Delta NPV = NPV(P) - NPV(L) =$$

$$\sum_{t=1}^{N} \frac{(T(D_t) - O_t(1-T)}{(1+K)^t} + \frac{S(1-T)}{(1+K_s)^N} - C + \sum_{t=1}^{N} \frac{L_t(1-T)}{(1+K_d)^t} \qquad (5)$$

where Δ denotes the difference between NPV(P) and NPV(L). *A positive result indicates that ownership is the best decision; a negative result, that leasing is preferred. A positive result occurs if (1) net salvage value exceeds the cost of owning; or (2) the cost of the asset less the depreciation tax savings is less than the lease payments.* Expression (5) converts to simple arithmetic as follows:

Year	(1) Depreciation Tax Savings $T(D_t)$	(2) After-Tax Operating Cost $O(1-T)$	(3) $1-2$	(4) Discount Factor $K = 10\%$	(5) 3×4
1	$29,000	1,000	28,000	.909	$ 25,452
2	19,140	1,000	18,140	.826	14,984
3	9,860	1,000	9,860	.751	7,405
Total					$ 47,841

Add
Present value of salvage: $4,000 × .579 (3 years @ 20%)   2,316
Total $ 50,157

Less
Cost of asset (I) $120,000
Total   ($69,843)
Add present value of leasing:

Year	(1) After-Tax Cost of Leasing $L_t(1-T)$	(2) Discount Factor $K_d - 3\%$ After Tax	(3) 1 × 2	
1	$23,660	.971	$22,974	
2	23,660	.943	22,311	
3	23,660	.915	21,649	66,934
NPV				($2,909)

Since the result is negative, leasing is the preferred alternative and improves NPV by $2,909. However, since purchase has a negative NPV of $8,444 this is not a sufficient improvement and the project should be abandoned. Note this second approach, viewing leasing and ownership as two separate projects, makes no assumptions as to how the asset will be acquired if owned—by borrowing, cash purchase, installment sale, etc. Hence interest is not included as an expense or tax saving. The after-tax effect of interest is accomplished by discounting the costs of ownership by the firm's cost of capital (K_{mc}). Figure 7-2 presents the schematic of the cash flows under the lease project approach.

Effective Interest Cost Method

The firm may wish to express its preference for leasing or ownership in terms of an interest cost associated with each. The procedure would hold true where the company views the alternatives as simply different methods of financing and where it wishes to assess the impact of its choice on the cost of capital.

Figure 7–2.   Cash Flow Sequence: Lease Project Approach

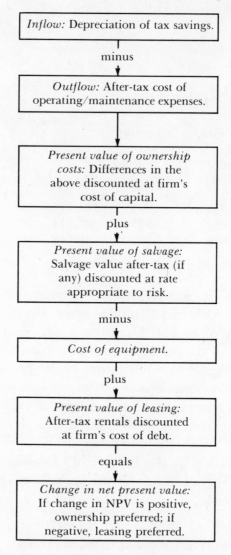

Inflow: Depreciation of tax savings.

minus

Outflow: After-tax cost of operating/maintenance expenses.

Present value of ownership costs: Differences in the above discounted at firm's cost of capital.

plus

Present value of salvage: Salvage value after-tax (if any) discounted at rate appropriate to risk.

minus

Cost of equipment.

plus

Present value of leasing: After-tax rentals discounted at firm's cost of debt.

equals

Change in net present value: If change in NPV is positive, ownership preferred; if negative, leasing preferred.

The effective before-tax interest cost (i) of ownership is that discount rate which equates the cash outflows (payment on loan plus operating expenses) before tax to the purchase cost (C) of the asset. The before-tax rate is then reduced by the firm's tax rate to secure the effective after-tax interest cost.

Apropos of the asset cost (C), since the discounted salvage value would reduce the cash outflows (i.e., lower the internal rate), the same effect is achieved by adding the present value of the salvage (S) to the cost of the equipment. The expression for ownership becomes:

$$C + S = GO \times \sum_{t=1}^{N} \frac{1}{(1+i)^t} \qquad (6)$$

where:

GO = gross ownership cost before tax (payment on loan plus operating expenses)

S = present value of salvage

i = effective interest cost. Solve for i.

Using the same data as in the cost minimization approach (see page 93) payment on loan plus operating expenses equals $37,174.

Step 1—Effective Interest Cost of Ownership

$$\$200,000 + \$1,080 = \$37,174 \times \sum_{t=1}^{10} \frac{1}{(1+i)^t} \qquad (7)$$

$$201,080 = \$37,174X$$

$$X = 5.4096 \text{ (Interest Factor)}$$

Then, solving for i using Table A-1 in the Appendix, an interest factor of 5.410 falls between 13 percent and 14 percent for a 10-year interval:

$$13\% = 5.426$$
$$X = 5.410$$
$$14\% = 5.216$$

From this comparison the interest rate is seen to be just over 13 percent. A more accurate answer requires that we interpolate, as follows:

$$5.426 - 5.216 = .210$$

and

$$5.426 - 5.410 = .016$$

Therefore, the correct interest rate is .016/.210 of the distance between 13 percent and 14 percent:

$$\frac{.016}{.210} = .076 \text{ (percent)}$$

$13\% + .076\% = 13.076\%$ effective interest cost of ownership *pretax*

The after-tax interest rate is $(1 - T)$ times this percentage; since the assumed tax rate is 50 percent,

$13.076\% \times .50 = .065$ effective interest cost of ownership *after tax*

Step 2—Effective Interest Cost of Leasing: Rent Paid at End of Period ($35,397)

$$C = L_t \times \sum_{t=1}^{N} \frac{1}{(1+i)^t} \tag{8}$$

$$\$200,000 = \$35,397 \times \sum_{t=1}^{10} \frac{1}{(1+i)^t}$$

$$200,000 = \$35,397X$$

$$X = 5.650$$

Then, solving for i using Table A–1 in the Appendix, an interest factor of 5.650 falls in the 12 percent, ten-year column. Hence

.12 = Effective interest cost of leasing *pretax*

50% × .12 = .06 effective interest cost of leasing *after tax*

Leasing is preferred by 1 percent (13 percent versus 12 percent) *pretax*, and by ½ percent (6.5 percent versus 6 percent) *posttax*.

Step 3—Effective Interest Cost of Leasing: Rent Paid in Advance ($30,000)

$$C = L_o + L_t \times \sum_{t=0}^{N} \frac{1}{(1 + i)^t} \tag{9}$$

$$\$200,000 = \$30,000 + \$30,000 \times \sum_{t=0}^{9} \frac{1}{(1 + i)^t}$$

$$\$200,000 - \$30,000 = \sum_{t=0}^{9} \frac{\$30,000}{(1 + i)^9} \ \ or \ \$170,000 = \$30,000X$$

$$X = 5.6667$$

Then, solving for i using Appendix Table A-2:

Trying 12% for 9 years yields an IF of 5.650 ⌉
Expression (9) yields IF of 5.667   ⌡ = .017 ⌉
Trying 11% for 9 years yields IF of 5.537   ⌡ = .113

Then

$$\frac{.017}{.113} \times .01 = .0015$$

and

.11 + .0015 = .1115 = .112 effective interest cost of leasing pre-tax ⎫
.112 × .50 = .056 effective interest cost of leasing post-tax ⎬ i
⎭

Leasing once again has a lower effective interest cost.

Summary

This chapter has presented three methods of analysis from the lessee's perspective. *All are valid*. Whether the potential lessee selects one or the other depends upon whether the assumptions of the model fit the circumstances of the firm's situation. If the firm has already decided to acquire the asset and is interested in leasing or ownership only as a financing problem, then the first approach is warranted. If no decision has been made on acquisition, then leasing and ownership may be viewed as separate projects and the second approach employed. The third approach has the same assumptions as the first but states the result in terms of effective interest cost.

Finally, a word of caution. This chapter stresses financial analysis. The techniques illustrated will make the correct decision based upon cash flows. Of course, the *results* of the decision to lease or buy will eventually be reported in conventional accounting statements, and the accepted accounting measures of income will differ in amount and timing from the income measures developed in a sound financial analysis. Although there may sometimes seem to be conflict among these different sets of requirements, *in the long run* the firm does better by putting into effect the decision indicated by a financial analysis of cash flows. After all, the market value of the firm derives from the timing, amount, and uncertainty attached to its future cash flows.

CHAPTER 8

The Special Case of Leveraged Leases: Measuring Profitability after Taxes

Bole and Ahlstrom define a leveraged lease as

the acquisition of an item of capital equipment for a period equal to most, but not all, of its anticipated economic life and the sale of the residual value and tax benefits of ownership to another party in exchange for a lease rate that is lower than the debt rate that would have applied to a purchase of the equipment.[1]

In its present form leveraged leasing is largely the product of government policies. Commencing with the Internal Revenue Code of 1954, successive tax regulations sought to stimulate private investment in personal property by (1) accelerated depreciation allowances and (2) investment tax credits. In 1963, the United States Comptroller of the Currency authorized national banks to own and lease property. Similar regulatory changes for state-chartered banks soon followed. These rulings in combination created the economic foundation for the leveraged leasing movement. *In essence they permitted banks and other financial institutions (or individuals) that had taxable income but lacked commensurate tax deductions to enter upon lease arrangements with companies seeking capital equipment and having the tax deductions but lacking suffi-*

cient taxable income to take advantage of them. Hence banks, other financial institutions, or individuals who might have no business use for particular capital assets had the economic incentive to invest in such capital assets and pass on some of the savings in the form of lower rentals to companies which might otherwise forgo the investment. Congress sought to foster economic growth by encouraging new investment and replacement of capital assets.

Parties to a Leveraged Lease

A leveraged lease frequently involves seven parties:

1.   *Owners*. These may include a consortium of commercial banks, insurance companies, finance companies, leasing companies, and/or individuals seeking the benefits of ownership, investment tax credits, accelerated depreciation, interest tax savings, and any residual value. Title to the property, as in all leases, rests with the owners.

2.   *Owner trustee*. The participating owners, rather than hold title directly, frequently appoint a trustee to hold the title for their benefit. The owner trustee (usually a commercial bank) also holds the owners' investment, which varies from a minimum of 20 percent to 50 percent of the equipment cost plus any legal costs and commissions to third parties for their services in arranging the deal. Upon receipt of the owner's investment, the trustee raises the balance of the purchase cost by selling creditor instruments to third parties.

3.   *Creditors*. The owner trustee raises the balance of the purchase cost by a private placement of debt with institutional leaders—for example, insurance companies and pension funds. A public sale by the trustee of debt would incur the expense of SEC registration and other costs involved in selling securities to the public. Consequently, public distribution takes place only when the debt is guaranteed by the U.S. government. In the latter case, the government mandates a public offering. In any event, the debt raised by the owner trustee

constitutes a *nonrecourse loan: the lenders agree to look for payment only to the lessee rental payments or, in case of default, to their lien on the capital equipment. They concede all recourse to the assets of the owner trustee or the participating owners.* The creditors look solely to the lessee for the debt service. *The credit of the lessor is de facto removed from the transaction.*

4. *Indenture trustee.* In view of the nonrecourse nature of the debt, the lenders may appoint an indenture trustee (usually a commercial bank) to guard their interests vis-à-vis the lessee and in repossession should default take place.

5. *Manufacturer or supplier.* After receiving the owner's investment and the funds from the sale of the creditor instruments, the owner trustee purchases the asset from the manufacturer, supplier, or contractor. He then arranges the lease of the equipment.

6. *Lessee.* The term of the lease is usually made identical with the amortization period of the debt. The rentals usually fall due on the day preceding the payment of the debt service. However, at times the lease may run one or two years longer than the repayment of the debt to give the owners the benefit of additional cash flow.

7. *Guarantor. Since the owners are effectively removed from liability to the creditors by the terms of the lease, the financial viability of the arrangement depends upon the credit standing of the lessee. If this appears inadequate, a guarantor may be sought to back up the lessee's undertakings.* The guarantor may be the parent company or affiliate of the lessee firm, a major customer of the lessee, or the lessee's commercial bank. Governmental agencies also act as guarantors for particular types of lease arrangements that contribute to the attainment of their objectives, e.g., the Export-Import Bank or the Maritime Administration.[2]

Figure 8-1 diagrams the relationship of the parties.

Manifestly, the construction of a leveraged lease is a complex deal to negotiate and document. But the essential motivations are easy to grasp. The lessor (owners) *by investing 20*

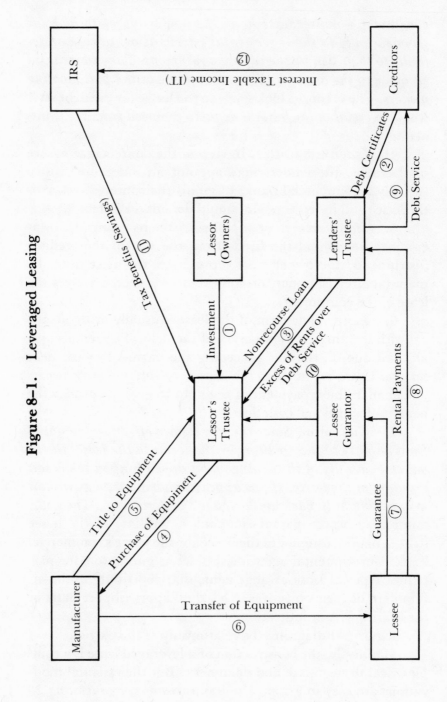

Figure 8-1. Leveraged Leasing

percent of the purchase cost captures 100 percent of the investment tax credits, the tax savings on accelerated depreciation, the tax savings on the debt service, and the residual value, if any. The lessor would also enjoy the earnings from the investment of the tax savings from accelerated depreciation. These "goodies" permit theoretical after-tax yields on the equity of 30 to 50 percent, part of which can be returned to the lessee in lower rentals. *Hence the lessee acquires a capital asset at a rental cost lower than the debt service he would pay if he acquired the equipment by borrowing*—usually 3 to 4 points less. The creditors get a high-quality security backed by a high collateral ratio, with the right of repossession in the event of default. Moreover, the debt security may be guaranteed by a third party. This is not to say there are no risks to the parties involved.

Lessor's Risks

If the lessee defaults and the lenders repossess the equipment pursuant to their lien, the lessor stands to lose some fraction of his investment (less the investment tax credit) plus the tax savings he would have enjoyed from the accelerated depreciation and the after-tax residual value of the asset.

Since so many of the advantages to leveraged leasing depend on tax legislation, changes in the Internal Revenue Code may adversely affect the lessor's position. For example, an increase in the tax rate during the term of the lease means that the tax savings taken at the lower rate would need to be paid back at a higher rate.

The lessor also runs the risk of not having a net taxable income from other activities to take advantage of the deductions allowed over the term of the lease.

Lender's Risk

The presence of a guarantor mitigates the lender's risk. So too does the lien on the property and the right of repossession. However, in the absence of a guarantor, the repossession of the property does not insure the lender against risk. The property may have suffered a serious decline in market value below the remaining debt, due to general economic conditions. Also, if the lessee could not make a go of the asset, is it likely that the lenders with less expertise in the industry will do so? The fate of supertankers in the early 1970s constitutes a case in point. Moreover, one must bear in mind that a guarantee (even from government) is no better than the integrity and ability to pay of the guarantor.

Lessee's Risk

As noted above, a leveraged lease is sensitive to interest rate changes. The lessee signs the lease with the expectation that the rentals make for cheaper financing than could be had by borrowing and owning the asset directly. Consequently, if following the acceptance of the lease interest rates should fall, the lease in retrospect will look less attractive; i.e., the lessee's cost of financing will be higher than it might have been. On the other hand, the interest rate risk is not unique to leveraged leasing, but applies to all debt instruments issued at a fixed interest rate. Hindsight is always better than foresight.

A Historical Note

Basically, the main features of leveraged leasing are not novel. Their origins trace back to the 1870s, when railroads resorted to the Philadelphia Plan as a means of circumventing Pennsylvania law, which did not recognize the retention of title to personal property by a seller under a conditional bill of sale agreement as a defense against the claims of a buyer's creditors lacking knowledge of the contract (Figure 8-2). The Philadelphia Plan, by contrast, allowed a group of investors to contribute an amount of money (equal to

Figure 8-2. Philadelphia Plan

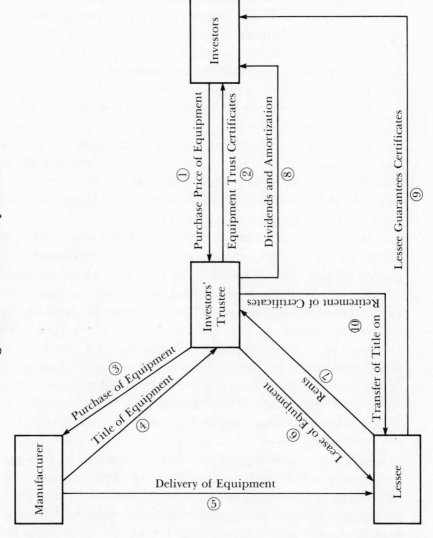

113

the purchase price of the equipment) to a commercial bank designated as trustee. Each investor received an *equipment trust certificate* from the trustee providing for the repayment of the face amount or principal plus a yield (called dividends) over a specified period of time. In typical arrangements, a trustee bank would then purchase the equipment from the manufacturer and in turn would lease the equipment to a railroad. The railroad generally would guarantee the certificates, thus giving the holders a right of direct action against the line.

Rental payments by the railroad would be timed to cover the amortization of the principal, payment of the dividends, and any expenses of the transaction. Moreover, the certificates would be paid off faster than the equipment depreciated, so that the ownership equity would build up over the term of the lease. At the conclusion of the lease when all the certificates were retired, title would pass to the railroad.

If during the term of the lease the railroad were to default or file in bankruptcy (a common disease of railroads), the trustee holding the title to the equipment would have the right to order the equipment assembled at a designated location and returned to his possession. For this reason the bankruptcy trustee, appointed by the Federal Court and charged with keeping the railroad running, generally would continue to make good on the equipment trust certificates as his first order of business. Under such arrangements the bankruptcy court in effect would guarantee the certificates.

A different approach was applied in states that enforced the conditional bill of sale against the claims of third parties lacking prior knowledge of the sale (Figure 8–3). This approach was called the New York Plan. In it the railroad took the initiative in obtaining investors to cover the cost of the property. The road then purchased the equipment from the manufacturer under a conditional bill of sale, payable in installments equal to the purchase price plus interest. The conditional bill of sale was then assigned by the manufacturer to the investors (or to their agent, such as a designated commercial bank) after receipt of the purchase price. Each investor received a participation certificate which called for repayment

Figure 8-3. New York Plan

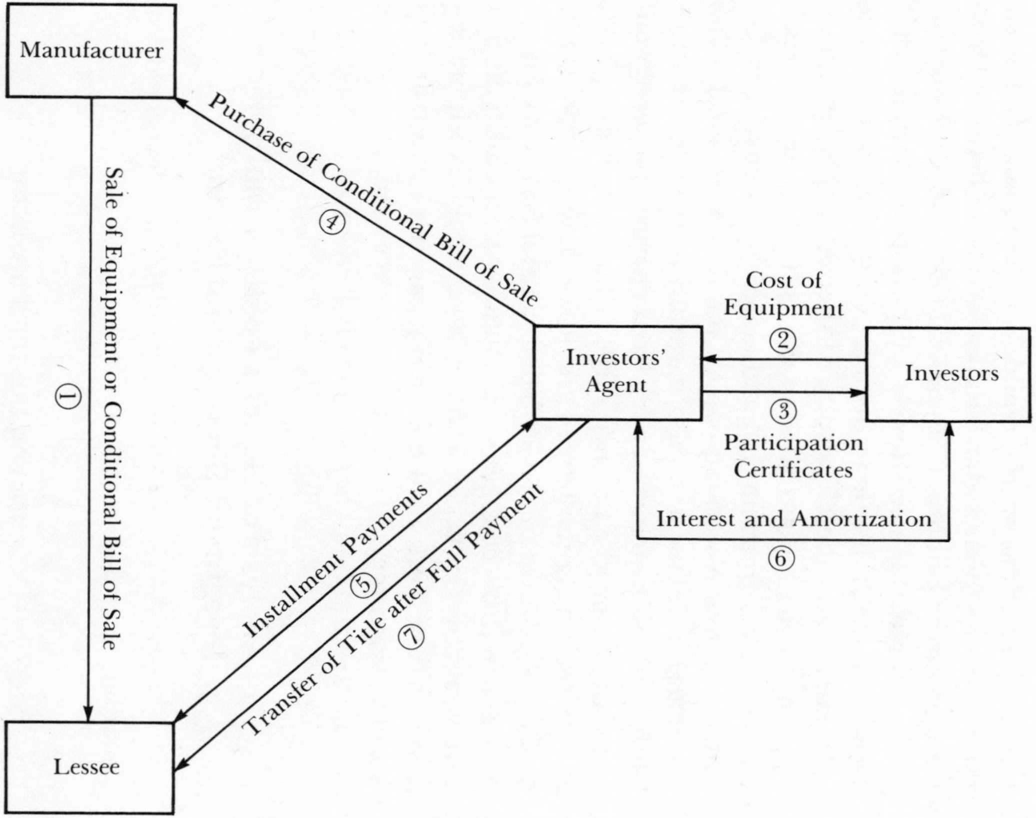

Investors

Cost of
Equipment
②

③ Participation
Certificates

⑥ Interest and Amortization

Investors'
Agent

④ Purchase of Conditional Bill of Sale

⑤ Installment Payments

⑦ Transfer of Title after Full Payment

Manufacturer

Sale of Equipment or Conditional Bill of Sale
①

Lessee

of principal and interest on a timetable concurrent with the railroad's installment schedule. Title to the equipment passed to the road with the final payment.

Neither the Philadelphia Plan nor the New York Plan allowed for "trading on the equity" or leveraging. Nor would they meet the qualifications today for a true lease under the tax laws or the Uniform Commercial Code, since the user (lessee) acquired the asset merely by paying the rental installments, secured full title to the asset on termination of the arrangement, and thereby captured the residual value. On the other hand, both plans allowed the railroad to escape restrictive covenants frequent in bond issues (maintenance of D/E ratios, minimum working capital requirements, etc.). While the rental installments would naturally appear on the lessee's profit and loss statement under fixed charges, the lease would not show up on the balance sheet as an asset or liability—in theory preserving the lessee's credit standing *ex ante*. Figures 8-2 and 8-3 illustrate the Philadelphia and New York Plans.

Spurred by changes in accounting standards, the Uniform Commercial Code, and tax laws, the Philadelphia Plan and the New York Plan eventually gave way to a true lease. Then the commercial banks and finance companies entered the picture and brought the added ingredient of leveraging.

Analysis of Lessor's Position: Multiple Investment Sinking Fund Method

To determine the lessor's yield in a leveraged lease situation, several steps are required:

Step 1—Determining Lessor's Investment

Assume a lessor plans to acquire an asset costing $1,000,000 (C) and put it out to lease. He plans to borrow $800,000 (D) and invest $200,000 (E). He would have to incur $15,000 in legal costs (LE) but would have an investment tax credit (ITC) of 10 percent. What is the lessor's investment?

Lessor's Equity Investment

Gross investment (E)	$200,000
Less	
Investment tax credit (ITC) (.10 × $1,000,000)	100,000
Net	$100,000
Plus	
Legal expenses (LE)	15,000
Lessor's investment (I)	$115,000

Note that the investment tax credit (ITC) is applied to the total cost of asset (C), not to the lessor's equity (I). Yet the lessor investing but $215,000 of his own funds receives the full $100,000 ITC. In cash flow terms, the situation at this point appears as follows:

Net cash outflows	$200,000 (E) (20% of cost)
	15,000 (LE)
Total	$215,000
Cash inflow	100,000 (ITC)
Net cash outflow	$115,000 (I)

Step 2—Determining Depreciation and Loan Service

Assume the lessor plans a ten-year lease; will depreciate the asset on an SYD basis over seven years; and will amortize the nonrecourse loan (P) over the full term of the lease, ten years (N). The loan has a nominal yield of 6 percent (R).

Sum of Years Digits (SYD)

Depreciation Schedule

$$SYD = \frac{N(N+1)}{2}$$

$$= \frac{7(7+1)}{2}$$

$$= \frac{56}{2}$$

$$= 28$$

Period (t)	Amount to Be Depreciated	SYD	Annual Depreciation (D)
1	$1,015,000	7/28	$ 253,750
2	1,015,000	6/28	217,500
3	1,015,000	5/28	181,250
4	1,015,000	4/28	145,000
5	1,015,000	3/28	108,750
6	1,015,000	2/28	72,500
7	1,015,000	1/28	36,250
			$1,015,000

Loan Amortization Schedule

$$\text{Annual payment} = P \times \sum_{t=1}^{N} \frac{1}{(1+R)^t}$$

$$= \$800,000 \times \sum_{t=1}^{10} \frac{1}{(1+.06)^t}$$

From Table A-1 in the Appendix, $\sum_{t=1}^{10} \frac{1}{(1+.06)^t} = 7.360$.

Therefore $800,000/7.360 gives the annual repayment on the nonrecourse loan, $108,696.

Year	Amortization	Principal	Interest	Balance
0				$800,000
1	$108,696	$ 60,696	$ 48,000	739,304
2	108,696	64,338	44,358	674,966
3	108,696	68,198	40,498	606,768
4	108,696	72,290	36,405	534,478
5	108,696	76,627	32,069	457,851
6	108,696	81,225	27,471	376,625
7	108,696	86,098	22,598	290,527
8	108,696	91,264	17,432	199,263
9	108,696	96,740	11,956	102,523
10	108,696	102,545	6,151	—
Total			$286,939	

Step 3—Lessor's Cash Flows

Assume the lessor can negotiate a $130,000 rental, payable at the end of the year. What is the cash flow pattern from the lease? The lessor's marginal tax rate (T) is 48 percent.

Year	Rent	Depreciation Expenses	Interest	Taxable Income	Tax Payment (T)
1	$ 130,000	$ 253,750	$ 48,000	− $171,750	− $82,440
2	130,000	217,500	44,358	− 131,858	− 63,292
3	130,000	181,250	40,498	− 91,748	− 44,039
4	130,000	145,000	36,406	− 51,406	− 24,675
5	130,000	108,750	32,069	− 10,819	− 5,193
6	130,000	72,500	27,471	+ 30,029	+ 14,414
7	130,000	36,250	22,598	+ 71,152	+ 34,153
8	130,000	0	17,432	+ 112,568	+ 54,033
9	130,000	0	11,956	+ 118,044	+ 56,661
10	130,000	0	6,151	+ 123,849	+ 59,448
	$1,300,000	$1,015,000	$286,939	+ $ 1,930	+ $ 930

If the lessor has substantial tax obligations from other sources, the negative cash flows of years 1 to 5 become in effect cash inflows by reducing his total tax payout. A further reduction in his tax bill is obtained from the investment tax credit. *Considering the time value of money, the tax payments in the later years of the lease have a lower present value than do the tax reductions in the earlier years of the lease, so that the economic benefits may be substantial. This condition generally characterizes leveraged leasing.*

Another feature worth observing is that the annual rentals ($130,000) are always greater than the debt service ($108,696). The rental incomes are fully taxable, but the interest portion of the debt service qualifies for a tax deduction. *Hence the lessor has income equal to the cash he receives from the difference between the rental income and the interest tax savings plus the debt principal.* If this sum only covers his own equity, he has income equal to his investment plus the debt principal. In the latter instance, he has depreciation deductions in the same amount and his tax liability is zero.

Finally, the most important part of the preceding table is that taxes are saved in the early years and paid in the later years, which enhances the present value of the lease.

In summary, the lessor's cash flow equals the tax payments saved plus the actual cash received (the excess of rentals over debt service). For year 1 in the present example this equals:

Rental	$130,000
Less Debt service	108,696
	$ 21,304
Plus Tax savings	82,440
Total	$103,744 (ignoring signs for the moment)

Summary of Lessor's Cash Inflows (+) and Outflows (−), Prepared Using the Above Analysis of Lessor Cash Flows:

Period (t)		Cash Flows	
0	Investment	− $200,000	
	Legal expenses	− 15,000	
1	ITC	+ 100,000	
1		+ 103,744	
2		+ 84,596	In each period these
3		+ 65,343	cash flows are the
4		+ 45,979	rental income less
5		+ 26,497	debt service plus tax
6		+ 6,890	savings, as developed
7		− 12,849	earlier (page 119)
8		− 32,729	
9		− 35,357	
10		− 38,144	
		+ $ 98,970	

Step 4—Determining Lessor's Rate of Return

The lessor has recaptured most of his investment by the
end of the first year and by the end of the tenth year has a cash
surplus of $98,970 after taxes. *The surplus of cash to the lessor
before the payment of taxes is termed the sinking fund.*

One method for determining the lessor's yield is the multiple investment sinking fund method (MISF). The method
uses one rate for the investment stage (the yield rate) and another rate for the sinking fund stage (the sinking fund rate). It
is a variation of the internal rate of return method. Disaggre-
gating the cash flow on this basis gives the following schedule:

Period	Total Cash Flows	Investment Balance	Investment Repay	Investment Earnings 38.895%	Sinking Fund	Sinking Fund Earns 10% After Taxes
0	− $215,000	0	0	0	0	0
1	+ 203,744	$215,000	$120,120	$83,624	—	—
2	+ 84,596	94,880	47,692	36,904	—	—
3	+ 65,343	47,188	46,989	18,354	—	—
4	+ 45,979	199	199	77	$45,703	—
5	+ 26,497	0	0	9	76,771	$4,571
6	+ 6,890	0	0	0	91,338	7,677
7	− 12,849	0	0	0	87,624	9,135
8	− 32,729	0	0	0	63,658	8,763
9	− 35,357	0	0	0	34,668	6,367
10	− 38,144	0	0	0	0	3,467
	+ $313,970					

Study the preceding schedule in light of the following
comments:

1.   The lessor has taxable income from other sources. He
needs tax deductions. Hence the tax losses of the years 1
through 6 create cash inflows due to saving taxes which would
otherwise be due on other income of the lessor. If it were not
for this saving of tax payments, the leveraged lease would have
a negative net present value. Stated differently, the leveraged
lease is not an independent project—the case with the leases
discussed in Chapter 6—but a dependent project linked to the
existence of taxable income from other sources.

2.   The yield under MISF approach (38.895%) is the yield on the lessor's investment while he has an investment outstanding (through period 3). This yield should represent what the lessor can earn after taxes on the reinvestment of his earnings. It must reduce the lessor's investment to zero during the term of the lease and is always applied against the remaining investment balance.

3.   After the reduction of the investment ($215,000) to zero, the remaining cash inflows accumulate as a sinking fund. The sinking fund earns interest at the sinking fund rate, which represents what the lessor could earn after taxes if he invested these funds in other securities or income-earning assets. The sinking fund earnings are compounded back into the sinking fund. Therefore when the cash flows turn negative (year 7), the sinking fund will be drawn down to cover the taxes. The sinking fund and the earnings thereon reduce the negative cash flows to zero by the end of the lease term.

4.   The MISF technique, accordingly, has two rates, the investment yield rate and the sinking fund rate. The yield rate (38,895%) is the rate for which both the investment balance and the sinking fund are reduced to zero by the end of the lease. However, there is risk here for the lessor: he might not be able to invest the sinking fund at the same rate projected when the lease was signed and/or he might not be able to achieve the level of reinvestment earnings assumed by the lease. The lessor too must contend with the interest rate risk.

5.   Finally, the above analysis assumes cash flows are received and paid at the end of the period (one year). In practice, the computations generally are made on a monthly basis. This adds to the labor of calculation, but not to any change in technique.

Under FAS No. 13, the MISF approach in effect becomes a means of distributing the net earnings of the lease against the full term of the lease by applying income to the open years of investment. Using the same data as in the preceding illustration but altering the presentation to conform to FAS No.

13's pro forma example, the recording of book earnings becomes as shown in the table on p. 124.

Under FAS No. 13, MISF is a means to allocate income and tax effects to the periods of net positive investment.

Analysis of the Lessor's Position: Internal Rate of Return (IRR)

The internal rate of return method is the same technique illustrated in Chapter 4, except that it is *computed on the lessor's equity investment rather than the total cost of the asset.* * The internal rate of return, therefore, is that rate which will discount the cash flows in Step 3 above to equal the lessor's equity investment (E). It is found by trial and error. For example, trying 40 percent as a possible rate, the present value of the cash flows would be calculated from Table A–2 in the Appendix:

Internal Rate of Return on Equity Investment — 40%

Period (t)	Cash Flow		Interest Factor	Present Value of Cash Flows
1	+ $203,744	×	.714	+ $145,473
2	+ 84,596	×	.510	+ 43,144
3	+ 65,343	×	.364	+ 23,785
4	+ 45,979	×	.260	+ 11,954
5	+ 26,497	×	.186	+ 4,928
6	+ 6,890	×	.133	+ 916
7	− 12,849	×	.095	− 1,221
8	− 32,729	×	.068	− 2,226
9	− 35,357	×	.048	− 1,697
10	− 38,144	×	.035	− 1,335
	+ $313,970			+ 223,725

*Recall that while the cost of the equipment is $1,000,000 the lessee or other party guarantees the $800,000 of debt financing. The lessor, accordingly, has a risk investment of only $200,000 plus legal expenses.

Year	Investment Balance Begin Yr.	Cash Flows*	Alloc. to Investment†	Alloc. to Income 31.56%†	Pretax Income	Tax Effects of P. Tax	ITC
1	+ $215,000	+ $203,744	+ $135,889	+ $67,855	− $1,323	− $635	+ $ 68,561
2	+ 79,111	+ 84,596	+ 59,629	+ 24,967	− 487	234	+ 25,227
3	+ 19,482	+ 65,343	+ 59,195	+ 6,148	− 120	58	+ 6,212
4	− 39,713	+ 45,979	+ 45,979	—	—	—	—
5	− 85,692	+ 26,497	+ 26,497	—	—	—	—
6	− 112,189	+ 6,890	+ 6,890	—	—	—	—
7	− 119,079	− 12,849	− 12,849	—	—	—	—
8	− 106,230	− 32,729	− 32,729	—	—	—	—
9	− 73,501	− 35,357	− 35,357	—	—	—	—
10	− 38,144	− 38,144	− 38,144	—	—	—	—
		+ $313,970	+ $215,000	+ $98,970	− $1,930	− $927‡	+ $100,000

*Per FAS No. 13 method these are the cash flows net of the original investment.

†The rate is that rate which when applied to the net investment in the years when the net investment is positive will distribute the net income (net cash flow) to those years. The rate is determined through trial and error. The rate must result in a total net income equal to the net cash flows, i.e., $98,970; see page 121.

‡Each component is allocated among the years of positive net investment in proportion to the allocation of net income (or loss), i.e., − $1,930 on page 119.

For example:

$\frac{\$67,855}{\$98,970} \times (\$1,930) = (\$1,323)$; $(\$1,323) \times .48 = (\$635)$

Or,

$\frac{\$67,855}{\$98,970} \times \$100,000 = \$68,561$

Since the present value of the cash flows (+ $223,723) exceeds the lessor's equity ($215,000), a 40 percent rate is too low. Try 45 percent.

Internal Rate of Return on Equity Investment—45%

Period (t)	Cash Flow		Interest Factor	Present Value of Cash Flows
1	+ $203,744	×	.690	+ $140,583
2	+ 84,596	×	.476	+ 40,268
3	+ 65,343	×	.328	+ 21,433
4	+ 45,979	×	.226	+ 10,391
5	+ 26,497	×	.156	+ 4,134
6	+ 6,890	×	.108	+ 744
7	− 12,849	×	.074	− 951
8	− 32,792	×	.051	− 1,669
9	− 35,357	×	.035	− 1,237
10	− 38,144	×	.024	− 915
	+ $313,970			+ 212,780

The 45 percent rate places the present value of the cash flows below $215,000. We know the correct internal rate must lie between 40 and 45 percent. Interpolating to find the true rate:

	Rate	PV of Cash Flows
	(.40	$223,723
	(	
.05	(?	215,000
	(	
	(.45	212,780

$$\$223,723 - \$212,780 = \$10,943$$
$$\$223,723 - \$215,000 = \$ 8,723$$

$$\frac{\$ 8,723}{\$10,943} \times .05 = .04$$

Hence .40 + .04 = 44% internal rate of return on equity. If the internal rate of return exceeds the lessor's marginal cost of capital (IRR > K_{mc}), the lease is acceptable.

Some features of the IRR approach merit comment:

1. It gives only a single rate of return, i.e., 44 percent.

2. It assumes the investment earnings and sinking fund earnings are calculated at the same rate, i.e., 44 percent.

3. Accordingly, the IRR generally exceeds the yield rate under the MISF approach.

4. It is possible that the IRR method may result in multiple rates which will all discount the cash flows to equal the lessor's equity investment. Which rate is the appropriate rate in this case? The answer lies in selecting a rate which best approximates the company's actual return in reinvested earnings or in changing the analysis to a net present value basis using the company's after-tax cost of equity capital (K_{mc}) as the discount rate. To illustrate, suppose the company's after-tax capital is 20 percent; what is the NPV of the lease?

Net Present Value Approach — $K_{mc} = .20$

Period (t)	Cash Flow		Interest Factor	Present Value of Cash Flows
1	+ $203,744	×	.833	+ $169,719
2	+ 84,596	×	.694	+ 58,710
3	+ 65,343	×	.579	+ 37,834
4	+ 45,979	×	.482	+ 22,162
5	+ 26,497	×	.402	+ 10,652
6	+ 6,890	×	.335	+ 2,308
7	− 12,849	×	.279	− 3,585
8	− 32,729	×	.233	− 7,626
9	− 35,357	×	.194	− 6,859
10	− 38,144	×	.162	− 6,179

Total present value (PV)   + $277,136

Less

Lessor's equity (E)   215,000

Net present value   + $ 62,136

However, if the firm's (lessor's) marginal cost of capital (K_{mc}) were 10 percent, the NPV of the lease would fall to $3,774. Conversely, if K_{mc} rose, NPV would also increase. In summary, if

K_{mc} equaled:	NPV would equal:
20%	+ $62,136
25%	+ 47,924
35%	+ 21,010
40%	+ 8,721

The shape of the NPV profile reflects the nature of the cash flow stream. At very low discount rates, the negative cash flows in years 7 to 10 tend to lower the NPV, As the discount rate rises, these negative cash flows become less important and, at higher discount rates, the negative cash flows approach zero. NPV thus rises as the discount rate mounts—at least up to some point. Over the range 10 percent to 40 percent, NPV is positive with a peak NPV at 20 percent. Beyond 20%, the positive cash flows of years 1 to 6 are reduced as the discount rate (K_{mc}) rises. Beyond 40 percent, the NPVs would tend to turn negative. In any case, if the NPV were calculated on the total cost of the asset (C) of $1,015,000, a negative NPV would result.

In our illustration, the lessor would accept the leveraged lease with a discount of approximately 20%.

IRS Guidelines

Chapter 5 covered the tax aspects of leasing. Nevertheless, it seems appropriate at this point to recapitulate the tax rules governing leveraged leases:

1.   The lessor must have a minimum, unconditional investment of at least 20 percent of the total cost of the property at the start of the lease.

2.   The investment must be maintained during the term of the lease.

3.   The equipment must have a residual value at the end of the lease, and the lessor must bear the risk of this value.

4.   The residual value must be at least 20 percent of original cost at the end of the lease.

5. The equipment must not be leased for more than 80 percent of its economic life.

6. The lessor may not have the right or intention to acquire the property at less than its fair market value. No member of the lessee group may acquire the property for less than its fair market value.

7. No member of the lessee group may pay for part of the cost of the equipment.

8. No member of the lessee group may lend to the lessor any funds to acquire the property or guarantee any indebtedness related to the acquisition of the property by the lessor.

9. The lessor must show a profit on the lease apart from tax benefits; that is, the sum of the rent and residual value should exceed the debt service plus the equity investment.

10. The lessor must receive substantial cash flow from the lease; that is, the total rent must exceed the total debt service by at least 2 percent of the investment times the number of years in the lease.

11. Rents need not be set at a fixed annual amount if the annual rent is either (a) always within 10 percent of the average of the rentals or (b) within 10 percent of the average for at least the first two-thirds of the lease and for the remainder of the lease no higher than the highest rent during the initial portion of the term and no lower than half the average rent during the initial portion.

Summary

Leveraged leasing obviously has its principal attraction in the acquisition of costly assets: aircraft, ships, industrial plants, and expensive equipment items. This does not rule out smaller assets if the tax benefits to the parties make the deal attractive. In general, however, the increasing cost of capital flowing from complex technology plus the tax structure constitutes the foundation of the leveraged leasing movement.

Whether leveraged leasing is for you depends upon whether you have tax deductions without commensurate income or taxable income without sufficient tax deductions. If so, you might contact one of the major leasing corporations mentioned in Chapter 1.

CHAPTER 9

Basic Rules for Negotiating Leases

This chapter recapitulates the fundamentals of lease evaluation illustrated in the previous chapters in order to establish a set of guidelines for negotiating lease proposals:

1. *Cash flows.* Financial lease analysis, whether by the lessor or lessee, looks to the cash benefits (sales inflows and/or cash savings in operating expenses, etc.) and cash outflows (interest payments, rentals, operating expenses, etc.) *which arise only from the existence of the lease and which would disappear if the lease disappeared.* Noncash items (depreciation, for example) are significant for the cash tax savings which they generate.

2. *Key variables.* Review the lease proposal for the cash values and/or tax savings associated with the key variables—common to all lease projects—described in Chapter 4. Stated differently, read the lease contract paragraph by paragraph asking the question, Does this represent a cash outflow or inflow? Is the particular cash flow (inflow or outflow) a fixed obligation or a contingent obligation, i.e., dependent upon the occurrence of some other event (change in tax laws, breach of warranty, etc.)? This helps in assessing the amount of risk inherent in the lease agreement.

3. *Type of lease.* As a corollary to 2, determine the tax classification of the lease—financial lease, operating lease, maintenance lease, leveraged lease, and so forth. IRS has es-

tablished criteria for a true lease (rentals are fully tax deductible) and a disguised lease or conditional bill of sale. In the latter case the *buyer* is the property's equitable owner and may deduct depreciation and interest expenses appropriate to ownership. The classification of the lease also relates to the accounting presentation on the firm's financial statements discussed below.

4. *Mandatory or discretionary acquisition.* The issues here relate to the analytical frameworks described in Chapter 7 and are mainly pertinent to the lessee. Is the asset to be acquired a mandatory investment, as with environmental equipment, or has the decision been made to obtain the asset after prior assessment of its profitability? If this is the case, the single question remaining is to find the lowest-cost method of financing—that is, to find whether it is cheaper to lease or borrow and buy. This is the question treated in discussion of the cost minimization approach in Chapter 7. On the other hand, if no decision has been made regarding the acquisition, then the lessee may treat leasing as one project and ownership as a separate project and compare the two in terms of net present value. This approach typifies the second model in Chapter 7. Looking at ownership and leasing as separate projects has the advantage of *highlighting the possibility that an acquisition which may not appear desirable if purchased may look good if negotiated as a lease, or vice versa.* This is another way of stating a basic rule of capital budgeting; namely, *identify all alternatives.* Remember, you always have the alternative of not acquiring the asset at all. The net cash benefit (in relation to risk) has to justify the investment. Careful analysis of all alternatives within the firm may show the risk-return on the asset does not warrant its acquisition by lease or purchase.

5. *A lease is a forecast.* A lease concerns *future cash inflows and outflows.* The future is always uncertain, and therefore the cash estimates will generally be off the mark in some degree. This uncertainty creates risk. The greatest risk probably attaches to salvage values, but operating expenses and maintenance outlays may change. Rents conversely are usually

fixed once the agreement is signed. Inflation is a risk affecting all contracts. *The different cash flows, accordingly, must be discounted for time at a rate which reflects the degree of uncertainty surrounding the estimates.* Thus rent may be discounted at the lowest rate, the firm's after-tax cost of debt. Maintenance and operating expenditures subject to wider fluctuations might be discounted at the firm's marginal cost of capital (K_{mc}). Salvage values, subject perhaps to even greater risk, would be discounted at a rate greater than the firm's marginal cost of capital. Some authorities argue that since tax laws and market interest rates are subject to change, the conservative posture would dictate that *all* cash flows be discounted at the firm's marginal cost of capital (K_{mc}), albeit with the exception of salvage values discounted at a higher rate.

6. *Put yourself in the other fellow's position.* Chapters 6 and 7 described the analysis used by lessors and lessees in deciding on the acceptance of a lease. *Know the important variables on which the other party will base his decision.* This knowledge will enhance your capacity to bargain for a more favorable deal. You are both bargaining from estimates, which implies there is room for compromise if you know the questions to ask and the possible trade-offs. The rule applies especially to leveraged leasing, which involves more than two parties.

7. *Special case of the lessor-manufacturer.* The lessor-manufacturer must decide where his advantage lies—in selling or leasing his product. To do this, he must first determine what rental will give him the same net present value as would result from selling the product. From this point he can adjust the rental or the selling price to encourage sale or leasing.

8. *Accounting statements.* The classification of the lease for accounting and tax purposes has ramifications beyond the amounts payable to IRS. If the lease be a true financial lease and under accounting convention required to be capitalized and reflected as an asset and liability on the firm's balance sheet, it will affect the debt/equity ratio. Frequently, bank loan agreements and bond indentures specify a debt/

equity ratio to be maintained by the firm. If you have one of these agreements, check into it or you may unwittingly find that you have violated the agreement. In other words, *the accounting treatment of the lease can influence your credit standing*.

The questions to be asked are numerous. The following checklist may assist you in contemplating the viability of the lease offer for your firm.

I.   Basic information
   A.   Has the project been evaluated independently by NPV and/or IRR?
   B.   Is the project acceptable on the above basis?
   C.   Is the issue to determine only the least-cost method of financing?
   D.   Will the purchase and lease alternatives be treated as independent projects?
   E.   Is the lease a capital or operating lease?
      1.   Does the lease transfer title of the property to the lessee at the end of the lease term?
      2.   Is there a purchase option?
      3.   Does the lease term cover 75 percent of the economic life of the leased property?
      4.   Will the fair value of the property decline at least 75 percent over the lease term?
      5.   Is there a sale and leaseback arrangement?
      6.   Check IRS guidelines for leveraged leasing.
      7.   Check IRS guidelines for a true lease versus conditional bill of sale.
      8.   Is the lease agreement affected by the terms of existing debt contracts?
      9.   Will the lease be capitalized for financial statement presentation?
     10.   Does the lessor absorb operating and/or maintenance charges on leased assets?
     11.   Is the lease renewable? On what terms?
   F.   Who gets the investment tax credit?
   G.   What method of depreciation is used?

H.   If the asset is acquired, are other assets to be liquidated, and what are the liquidation values?

I.   Is an additional working capital investment required?

J.   What is the estimated salvage value?

K.   What is the useful economic life of the asset?

L.   What is the trend of interest rates?

M.   Are there pending changes in tax legislation relating to lease arrangements?

N.   What are the expected additional sales or savings in expense items if the asset is acquired?

O.   Have you estimated your marginal cost of capital?

P.   What are the additional manufacturing, selling, and administrative expenses traceable to the lease?

Q.   What is your marginal tax rate?

R.   If purchased, how will the asset be financed?
   1. Term loan and rate?
   2. Long-term debt and rate?
   3. Preferred or common stock?
   4. Retained earnings?

S.   If leased:
   1. What is the annual rental?
   2. Are rents payable in advance? At the end of each period?
   3. Are operating costs, service charges, and maintenance costs absorbed by the lessor?
   4. Estimation of lessor's tax position?
   5. Maximum rental lessee will pay?
   6. Term of lease? Initial term and renewable period?

II.   Analysis of Purchase Alternative
   A.   Based upon cash flow:
      1. Evaluate purchase as *independent project*:
         a. What is the investment outlay?
         b. Project cash inflows and outflows for each period over the life of the project?

    c.   Determine net inflow (or outflow) per period and put on after-tax basis.

    d.   Does the discount factor reflect the reliability of the cash flows?

    e.   What is NPV?

    f.   What is the IRR?

    g.   Relating to item c above:

        (1) Set up amortization schedule for principal and interest if asset financed by purchase.

        (2) Set up operating, maintenance, and service charges per period.

        (3) Add up tax deductions for each period.

        (4) Estimate net ownership costs per period.

        (5) Estimate salvage value and working capital investment returnable at end of project.

        (6) What is present value advantage of ownership at after-tax cost of debt? At firm's marginal cost of capital?

    h.   Determine the resulting accounting income by developing the impact of cash flow analysis on accounting net income before and after taxes, considering especially the following items:

        (1) Tax versus book depreciation

        (2) Other accrual items

        (3) Return on assets (ROA)

        (4) Effect on working capital ratios

        (5) Effect on debt equity ratio

III.   Analysis of lease alternative

   A.   Based upon cash flow:

      1.   Evaluate lease as independent project: additional revenues and/or savings in expenses per period traceable to the project?

      2.   Annual rental and other expenses not assumed by lessor?

      3.   Loss of tax shields and residual values enjoyed by ownership?

   4. Net present value of leasing?
   5. Evaluate project with regard to method of
      financing:
      a. Annual rentals after tax?
      b. Other after-tax costs of leasing?
      c. Present value of leasing at after-tax cost of
         debt? At firm's marginal cost of capital?
   6. Determine the resulting accounting income by
      developing the impact of cash flow analysis on
      accounting net income before and after taxes.
IV. Area of negotiation
   A. Maximum rental lessee willing to pay?
   B. Flexibility in estimates on residuals, finance
      charges, operating expenses, and tax shields?
   C. Lessee's tax position? His marginal tax rate? Can
      he take advantage of investment tax credit and
      accelerated depreciation?
   D. Estimate lessor's tax position. Will change in
      lessor's tax position over course of lease affect the
      rental charges?
   E. Minimum rental the lessor is willing to accept.
V. Other factors affecting lease v. buy decision
   A. Will technology change in the foreseeable future?
   B. Will leasing or ownership require organizational
      changes?

For the businessman, know the questions and make others
work for you.

Notes

Chapter 1

1. These comments assume the lessor underestimates the rate of inflation and the trend of interest rates. Actually, if the price level were stabilized or declining, the rental—as with all debt payments —would seem more onerous to carry.

2. James H. McLean, "Economic and Accounting Aspects of Lease Financing." *Financial Executive*, 31 (December 1963), p. 23

Chapter 3

1. The lessor (owner of the asset) may use the straight line method for conventional accounting purposes and accelerated depreciation for tax purposes. The accounting treatment of accelerated depreciation is illustrated later in the chapter and discussed in detail in Chapter 2.

2. Of course the owner would receive the $10,000 in salvage at the end of the tenth year. However, this would not change the rankings. It would only add the same amount to each total.

3. For a more detailed discussion of the legal variables in lease negotiation, see Chapter I of Bruce E. Fritch and Albert F. Reisman, *Equipment Leasing—Leveraged Leasing* (New York: Practicing Law Institute, 1977).

Chapter 4

1.   This section summarizes key sections of FAS No. 13, which is a highly specialized and complex document. Interested readers are urged to consult the original, except in the most straightforward cases.

2.   This is an abridged version of the example given in FAS No. 13, Appendix E.

Chapter 6

1.   Based upon Jack E. Gaumnitz and Allen Ford, "The Lease or Sell Decision," *Financial Management* (Winter 1978), pp. 69-74.

2.   Straight line depreciation is used to simplify the calculations. SYD or DDB methods (Chapter 3) can easily be substituted. Similarly, we assumed no salvage value (S_v) and hence no tax on disposal of the asset.

Chapter 8

1.   Quoted in Bruce E. Fritch and Albert F. Reisman, *Equipment Leasing—Leveraged Leasing* (New York: Practicing Law Institute, 1977), p. 365.

2.   Ibid., pp. 105-110.

Glossary

Accelerated (rapid write-off) depreciation represents several methods of depreciation which assign larger expenses to the earlier years of asset use and correspondingly lower amounts to the later years of asset use, such as straight line (SL) and sum of the years digits (SYD) depreciation.

ADR system, Class Life Asset Depreciation Range system, allows taxpayers to choose from a range of depreciation methods that are not more than 20 percent below or above IRS guideline lives.

Capital budgeting is a technique which analyzes profitability of a proposed project, based upon the *incremental* cash inflows and outflows which would occur if the project were added (or dropped).

Capital expenditure is the purchase of a long-lived asset (i.e., one expected to last beyond a single year).

Capital lease represents a lease meeting FAS #13 criteria, so that the lease payments, discounted for interest, must appear as an asset and a liability in the lessee's financial statements.

Conditional sales contract, or an installment sale of an asset, where each installment payment includes interest and repayment of principal; any gain or loss on the sale is recognized at the beginning of the contract.

Cost of capital is defined as a composite or weighted average figure reflecting the costs of the various types of debt and equity financing used by the firm.

Debt-equity ratio is a widely used measure of financial leverage, measured either as (1) total debt divided by total assets or (2) total debt divided by shareholder equity.

141

Deferred taxes   arise because of differences in the timing of revenues and expenses between financial accounting reports and tax returns, may be deferred tax debits or credits.

Depreciation   is a method of allocating the cost of using a long-lived asset to individual years. Over an asset's expected useful life total depreciation is measured as cost less salvage value.

Direct financing leases (FASB)   are leases that meet at least one of the FAS #13 standards for a capital lease and do not provide the lessor with a manufacturer or dealer profit at inception.

FASB   stands for the Financial Accounting Standards Board, the rule-making body of the financial accounting profession. Rules of the FASB are called Statements of Financial Accounting Standards (SFAS). The rules for reporting leases are detailed in SFAS No. 13.

Footnote   is an explanatory paragraph included with a firm's basic financial accounting statements, to offer additional information about operating results or financial position.

Internal rate of return   represents that rate used for discounting investment cash flows, so that the present value of the cash flows is equal to the cost of the investment.

Investment tax credit   is a credit against income taxes which is allowed to the owner of an asset, equal to 10 percent of the cost of eligible property placed in service during the tax year.

Lease   is an agreement conveying the right to use property, plant, or equipment for a stated period of time.

Leverage   represents the effect of fixed charges on the riskiness of cash flows. *Financial leverage* describes the effect of fixed interest payments (see also debt-equity ratio entry), while *operating leverage* describes the effect of other fixed expenses such as depreciation and amortization.

Leveraged lease (FASB)   constitutes a special form of direct financing lease involving a lessee, a lessor, and a long-term creditor who provides the major portion of financing for the leased asset, by issuing debt which is nonrecourse to the lessor.

Nonrecourse loan (in leverage leasing)   provides that in the event of default, the lenders agree to look for payment only to the lessee rental payments or to their lien on the leased equipment, and to have no recourse to the assets of the owners.

Operating lease   is a lease meeting *none* of the FAS #13 criteria for capital leases; basically, the lease covers only a portion of the asset's useful like, and the lessor bears the usual risks of ownership.

Owner trustee   in leverage leasing is a trustee appointed by the owners of the property to hold title for their benefit.

Present value   is the value today of money to be received at a future date, computed by discounting at a rate sufficient to allow for interest and risk.

Residual value   is estimated value of a leased asset at the end of the lease term.

Sale and leaseback   is an arrangement where the owner of property sells the property to a lessor, and the sales agreement requires that the property be leased back to the seller.

Sales-type leases (FASB)   provide a profit or loss to the lessor as a manufacturer of dealer, in addition to the income from leasing the asset.

Tax shield (tax shelter)   represents the reduction in taxes associated with a tax loss; tax losses in one type of activity (e.g., leasing) may be used to offset taxable gains in other areas of activity, provided the IRS guidelines are met.

Working capital   is the difference between a firm's short-term (or current) assets and current liabilities, often used as a measure of financial liquidity. Gross working capital is the total current assets.

Appendix

Notes to Table A–1

Table A-1 gives the present value of $1.00 *payable at the end of each period* for a specified number of periods at a given discount rate. For example, the present value of a $1.00 annuity payable in each of ten periods, discounted at 6 percent, equals $1.00 × 7.3601, or $7.36.

In the illustrating problems used in the various chapters, the table readings are rounded to three places. Thus 7.3601 becomes 7.360. However, if the last number were 8 instead of 1, the 0 would be raised to 1. Odd numbers followed by 5 are raised to the next higher digit; even numbers are not. All numbers followed by a digit greater than 5 are raised to the next higher value; all numbers followed by a digit less than 5 are left unchanged

Figure A–1.   Graphic Illustration of an Annuity: Present Value at 4% Interest

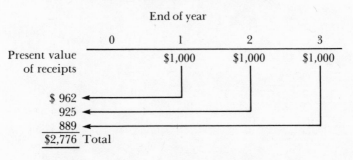

Table A–1.   Present Value of an Annuity of $1.00

n/r	38%	39%	40%	41%	42%	43%	44%	45%	46%	47%	48%	49%
1	0.7246	0.7194	0.7143	0.7092	0.7042	0.6993	0.6944	0.6897	0.6849	0.6803	0.6757	0.6711
2	1.2497	1.2370	1.2245	1.2122	1.2002	1.1883	1.1767	1.1653	1.1541	1.1430	1.1322	1.1216
3	1.6302	1.6093	1.5889	1.5689	1.5494	1.5303	1.5116	1.4933	1.4754	1.4579	1.4407	1.4239
4	1.9060	1.8772	1.8492	1.8219	1.7954	1.7694	1.7442	1.7195	1.6955	1.6720	1.6491	1.6268
5	2.1058	2.0699	2.0352	2.0014	1.9686	1.9367	1.9057	1.8755	1.8462	1.8177	1.7899	1.7629
6	2.2506	2.2086	2.1680	2.1286	2.0905	2.0536	2.0178	1.9831	1.9495	1.9168	1.8851	1.8543
7	2.3555	2.3083	2.2628	2.2189	2.1764	2.1354	2.0957	2.0573	2.0202	1.9842	1.9494	1.9156
8	2.4315	2.3801	2.3306	2.2829	2.2369	2.1926	2.1498	2.1085	2.0686	2.0301	1.9928	1.9568
9	2.4866	2.4317	2.3790	2.3283	2.2795	2.2326	2.1874	2.1438	2.1018	2.0613	2.0222	1.9844
10	2.5265	2.4689	2.4136	2.3605	2.3095	2.2605	2.2134	2.1681	2.1245	2.0825	2.0420	2.0030
11	2.5555	2.4956	2.4383	2.3833	2.3307	2.2801	2.2316	2.1849	2.1401	2.0969	2.0554	2.0154
12	2.5764	2.5148	2.4559	2.3995	2.3455	2.2938	2.2441	2.1965	2.1507	2.1068	2.0645	2.0238
13	2.5916	2.5286	2.4685	2.4110	2.3560	2.3033	2.2529	2.2045	2.1580	2.1134	2.0706	2.0294
14	2.6026	2.5386	2.4775	2.4192	2.3634	2.3100	2.2589	2.2100	2.1630	2.1180	2.0747	2.0331
15	2.6106	2.5457	2.4839	2.4249	2.3686	2.3147	2.2632	2.2138	2.1665	2.1211	2.0775	2.0357
16	2.6164	2.5509	2.4885	2.4290	2.3722	2.3180	2.2661	2.2164	2.1688	2.1232	2.0794	2.0374
17	2.6206	2.5546	2.4918	2.4319	2.3748	2.3203	2.2681	2.2182	2.1704	2.1246	2.0807	2.0385
18	2.6236	2.5573	2.4941	2.4340	2.3766	2.3219	2.2695	2.2195	2.1715	2.1256	2.0815	2.0393
19	2.6258	2.5592	2.4958	2.4355	2.3779	2.3230	2.2705	2.2203	2.1723	2.1263	2.0821	2.0398
20	2.6274	2.5606	2.4970	2.4365	2.3788	2.3238	2.2712	2.2209	2.1728	2.1267	2.0825	2.0401

n = number of time periods; r = rate of interest in percent.

Table A-1. (Cont.)

n/r	26%	27%	28%	29%	30%	31%	32%	33%	34%	35%	36%	37%
1	0.7937	0.7874	0.7813	0.7752	0.7692	0.7634	0.7576	0.7519	0.7463	0.7407	0.7353	0.7299
2	1.4235	1.4074	1.3916	1.3761	1.3609	1.3461	1.3315	1.3172	1.3032	1.2894	1.2760	1.2627
3	1.9234	1.8956	1.8684	1.8420	1.8161	1.7909	1.7663	1.7423	1.7188	1.6959	1.6735	1.6516
4	2.3202	2.2800	2.2410	2.2031	2.1662	2.1305	2.0957	2.0618	2.0290	1.9969	1.9658	1.9355
5	2.6351	2.5827	2.5320	2.4830	2.4356	2.3897	2.3452	2.3021	2.2604	2.2200	2.1807	2.1427
6	2.8850	2.8210	2.7594	2.7000	2.6427	2.5875	2.5342	2.4828	2.4331	2.3852	2.3388	2.2939
7	3.0833	3.0087	2.9370	2.8682	2.8021	2.7386	2.6775	2.6187	2.5620	2.5075	2.4550	2.4043
8	3.2407	3.1564	3.0758	2.9986	2.9247	2.8539	2.7860	2.7208	2.6582	2.5982	2.5404	2.4849
9	3.3657	3.2728	3.1842	3.0997	3.0190	2.9419	2.8681	2.7976	2.7300	2.6653	2.6033	2.5437
10	3.4648	3.3644	3.2689	3.1781	3.0915	3.0091	2.9304	2.8553	2.7836	2.7150	2.6495	2.5867
11	3.5435	3.4365	3.3351	3.2388	3.1473	3.0604	2.9776	2.8987	2.8236	2.7519	2.6834	2.6180
12	3.6059	3.4933	3.3868	3.2859	3.1903	3.0995	3.0133	2.9314	2.8534	2.7792	2.7084	2.6409
13	3.6555	3.5381	3.4272	3.3224	3.2233	3.1294	3.0404	2.9559	2.8757	2.7994	2.7268	2.6576
14	3.6949	3.5733	3.4587	3.3507	3.2487	3.1522	3.0609	2.9744	2.8923	2.8144	2.7403	2.6698
15	3.7261	3.6010	3.4834	3.3726	3.2682	3.1696	3.0764	2.9883	2.9047	2.8255	2.7502	2.6787
16	3.7509	3.6228	3.5026	3.3896	3.2832	3.1829	3.0882	2.9987	2.9140	2.8337	2.7575	2.6852
17	3.7705	3.6400	3.5177	3.4028	3.2948	3.1931	3.0971	3.0065	2.9209	2.8398	2.7629	2.6899
18	3.7861	3.6536	3.5294	3.4130	3.3037	3.2008	3.1039	3.0124	2.9260	2.8443	2.7668	2.6934
19	3.7985	3.6642	3.5386	3.4210	3.3105	3.2067	3.1090	3.0169	2.9299	2.8476	2.7697	2.6959
20	3.8083	3.6726	3.5458	3.4271	3.3158	3.2112	3.1129	3.0202	2.9327	2.8501	2.7718	2.6977

n/r	16%	17%	18%	19%	20%	21%	22%	23%	24%	25%
1	0.8621	0.8547	0.8475	0.8403	0.8333	0.8264	0.8197	0.8130	0.8065	0.8000
2	1.6052	1.5852	1.5656	1.5465	1.5278	1.5095	1.4915	1.4740	1.4568	1.4400
3	2.2459	2.2096	2.1743	2.1399	2.1065	2.0739	2.0422	2.0114	1.9813	1.9520
4	2.7982	2.7432	2.6901	2.6386	2.5887	2.5404	2.4936	2.4483	2.4043	2.3616
5	3.2743	3.1993	3.1272	3.0576	2.9906	2.9260	2.8636	2.8035	2.7454	2.6893
6	3.6847	3.5892	3.4976	3.4098	3.3255	3.2446	3.1669	3.0923	3.0205	2.9514
7	4.0386	3.9224	3.8115	3.7057	3.6046	3.5079	3.4155	3.3270	3.2423	3.1611
8	4.3436	4.2072	4.0776	3.9544	3.8372	3.7256	3.6193	3.5179	3.4212	3.3289
9	4.6065	4.4506	4.3030	4.1633	4.0310	3.9054	3.7863	3.6731	3.5655	3.4631
10	4.8332	4.6586	4.4941	4.3389	4.1925	4.0541	3.9232	3.7993	3.6819	3.5705
11	5.0286	4.8364	4.6560	4.4865	4.3271	4.1769	4.0354	3.9018	3.7757	3.6564
12	5.1971	4.9884	4.7932	4.6105	4.4392	4.2784	4.1274	3.9852	3.8514	3.7251
13	5.3423	5.1183	4.9095	4.7147	4.5327	4.3624	4.2028	4.0530	3.9124	3.7801
14	5.4675	5.2293	5.0081	4.8023	4.6106	4.4317	4.2646	4.1082	3.9616	3.8241
15	5.5755	5.3242	5.0916	4.8759	4.6755	4.4890	4.3152	4.1530	4.0013	3.8593
16	5.6685	5.4053	5.1624	4.9377	4.7296	4.5364	4.3567	4.1894	4.0333	3.8874
17	5.7487	5.4746	5.2223	4.9879	4.7746	4.5755	4.3908	4.2190	4.0591	3.9099
18	5.8178	5.5339	5.2732	5.0333	4.8122	4.6079	4.4187	4.2431	4.0799	3.9279
19	5.8775	5.5845	5.3162	5.0700	4.8435	4.6346	4.4415	4.2627	4.0967	3.9424
20	5.9288	5.6278	5.3527	5.1009	4.8696	4.6567	4.4603	4.2786	4.1103	3.9539

Table A-1. (Cont.)

n/r	6%	7%	8%	9%	10%	11%	12%	13%	14%	15%
1	0.9434	0.9346	0.9259	0.9174	0.9091	0.9009	0.8929	0.8850	0.8772	0.8696
2	1.8334	1.8080	1.7833	1.7591	1.7355	1.7125	1.6901	1.6681	1.6467	1.6257
3	2.6730	2.6243	2.5771	2.5313	2.4869	2.4437	2.4018	2.3612	2.3216	2.2832
4	3.4651	3.3872	3.3121	3.2397	3.1699	3.1024	3.0373	2.9745	2.9137	2.8550
5	4.2124	4.1002	3.9927	3.8897	3.7908	3.6959	3.6048	3.5172	3.4331	3.3522
6	4.9173	4.7665	4.6229	4.4859	4.3553	4.2305	4.1114	3.9975	3.8887	3.7845
7	5.5824	5.3893	5.2064	5.0330	4.8684	4.7122	4.5638	4.4226	4.2883	4.1604
8	6.2098	5.9713	5.7466	5.5348	5.3349	5.1461	4.9676	4.7988	4.6389	4.4873
9	6.8017	6.5152	6.2469	5.9952	5.7590	5.5370	5.3282	5.1317	4.9464	4.7716
10	7.3601	7.0236	6.7101	6.4177	6.1446	5.8892	5.6502	5.4262	5.2161	5.0188
11	7.8869	7.4987	7.1390	6.8051	6.4951	6.2065	5.9377	5.6869	5.4527	5.2337
12	8.3838	7.9427	7.5361	7.1607	6.8137	6.4924	6.1944	5.9176	5.6603	5.4206
13	8.8527	8.3577	7.9038	7.4869	7.1034	6.7499	6.4235	6.1218	5.8424	5.5831
14	9.2950	8.7455	8.2442	7.7862	7.3667	6.9819	6.6282	6.3025	6.0021	5.7245
15	9.7122	9.1079	8.5595	8.0607	7.6061	7.1909	6.8109	6.4624	6.1422	5.8474
16	10.1059	9.4466	8.8514	8.3126	7.8237	7.3792	6.9740	6.6039	6.2651	5.9542
17	10.4773	9.7632	9.1216	8.5436	8.0216	7.5488	7.1196	6.7291	6.3729	6.0472
18	10.8276	10.0591	9.3719	8.7556	8.2014	7.7016	7.2497	6.8399	6.4674	6.1280
19	11.1581	10.3356	9.6036	8.9501	8.3649	7.8393	7.3658	6.9380	6.5504	6.1982
20	11.4699	10.5940	9.8181	9.1285	8.5136	7.9633	7.4694	7.0248	6.6231	6.2593

n/r	5.0%	5.1%	5.2%	5.3%	5.4%	5.5%	5.6%	5.7%	5.8%	5.9%
1	.95238	.95147	.95057	.94967	.94877	.94787	.94697	.94607	.94518	.94429
2	1.85941	1.85678	1.85415	1.85154	1.84892	1.84632	1.84372	1.84113	1.83854	1.83597
3	2.72325	2.71815	2.71307	2.70801	2.70296	2.69793	2.69292	2.68792	2.68293	2.67797
4	3.54595	3.53773	3.52954	3.52138	3.51325	3.50515	3.49708	3.48904	3.48103	3.47305
5	4.32948	4.31753	4.30564	4.29381	4.28202	4.27028	4.25860	4.24697	4.23538	4.22385
6	5.07569	5.05950	5.04339	5.02736	5.01140	4.99553	4.97973	4.96402	4.94838	4.93281
7	5.78637	5.76546	5.74467	5.72399	5.70342	5.68297	5.66263	5.64240	5.62228	5.60228
8	6.46321	6.43717	6.41128	6.38555	6.35998	6.33457	6.30931	6.28420	6.25925	6.23445
9	7.10782	7.07628	7.04494	7.01382	6.98290	6.95220	6.92169	6.89139	6.86129	6.83139
10	7.72173	7.68437	7.64728	7.61046	7.57391	7.53763	7.50160	7.46584	7.43033	7.39508
11	8.30641	8.26296	8.21985	8.17708	8.13464	8.09254	8.05076	8.00931	7.96818	7.92737
12	8.86325	8.81347	8.76412	8.71517	8.66664	8.61852	8.57079	8.52347	8.47654	8.43000
13	9.39357	9.33727	9.28148	9.22619	9.17139	9.11708	9.06325	9.00991	8.95703	8.90463
14	9.89864	9.83566	9.77327	9.71148	9.65027	9.58965	9.52960	9.47011	9.41118	9.35281
15	10.37966	10.30985	10.24075	10.17234	10.10462	10.03758	9.97121	9.90550	9.84044	9.77602
16	10.83777	10.76104	10.68512	10.61001	10.53570	10.46216	10.38940	10.31740	10.24616	10.17566
17	11.27407	11.19033	11.10753	11.02565	10.94468	10.86461	10.78542	10.70710	10.62964	10.55303
18	11.68959	11.59879	11.50906	11.42037	11.33272	11.24607	11.16043	11.07578	10.99210	10.90938
19	12.08532	11.98744	11.89074	11.79523	11.70087	11.60765	11.51556	11.42458	11.33469	11.24587
20	12.46221	12.35722	12.25356	12.15121	12.05016	11.95038	11.85186	11.75457	11.65849	11.56362

Table A-1. (Cont.)

n/r	4.0%	4.1%	4.2%	4.3%	4.4%	4.5%	4.6%	4.7%	4.8%	4.9%
1	.96154	.96061	.95969	.95877	.95785	.95694	.95602	.95511	.95420	.95329
2	1.88609	1.88340	1.88070	1.87802	1.87534	1.87267	1.87000	1.86734	1.86469	1.86205
3	2.77509	2.76983	2.76459	2.75937	2.75416	2.74896	2.74379	2.73863	2.73349	2.72836
4	3.62990	3.62136	3.61285	3.60438	3.59594	3.58753	3.57915	3.57080	3.56249	3.55420
5	4.45182	4.43934	4.42692	4.41455	4.40224	4.38998	4.37777	4.36562	4.35352	4.34147
6	5.24214	5.22511	5.20818	5.19132	5.17456	5.15787	5.14127	5.12475	5.10832	5.09196
7	6.00205	5.97994	5.95794	5.93607	5.91433	5.89270	5.87120	5.84981	5.82855	5.80740
8	6.73274	6.70503	6.67749	6.65012	6.62292	6.59589	6.56902	6.54232	6.51579	6.48942
9	7.43533	7.40157	7.36803	7.33473	7.30165	7.26879	7.23616	7.20375	7.17156	7.13958
10	8.11090	8.07067	8.03074	7.99111	7.95177	7.91272	7.87396	7.83548	7.79729	7.75937
11	8.76048	8.71342	8.66674	8.62043	8.57449	8.52892	8.48371	8.43885	8.39436	8.35021
12	9.38507	9.33085	9.27710	9.22381	9.17097	9.11858	9.06664	9.01514	8.96408	8.91345
13	9.98565	9.92397	9.86286	9.80231	9.74231	9.68285	9.62394	9.56556	9.50771	9.45038
14	10.56312	10.49373	10.42501	10.35696	10.28957	10.22283	10.15673	10.09127	10.02644	9.96223
15	11.11839	11.04105	10.96450	10.88874	10.81376	10.73955	10.66609	10.59338	10.52141	10.45018
16	11.65230	11.56681	11.48225	11.39860	11.31586	11.23402	11.15305	11.07295	10.99372	10.91532
17	12.16567	12.07186	11.97912	11.88744	11.79680	11.70719	11.61859	11.53100	11.44438	11.35875
18	12.65930	12.55702	12.45597	12.35613	12.25747	12.15999	12.06367	11.96848	11.87441	11.78145
19	13.13394	13.02308	12.91360	12.80549	12.69873	12.59329	12.48916	12.38632	12.28475	12.18442
20	13.59033	13.47077	13.35278	13.23633	13.12139	13.00794	12.89595	12.78541	12.67628	12.56856

n/r	3.0%	3.1%	3.2%	3.3%	3.4%	3.5%	3.6%	3.7%	3.8%	3.9%
1	.97087	.96993	.96899	.96805	.96712	.96618	.96525	.96432	.96339	.96246
2	1.91347	1.91070	1.90794	1.90518	1.90244	1.89969	1.89696	1.89423	1.89151	1.88880
3	2.82861	2.82318	2.81777	2.81237	2.80700	2.80164	2.79629	2.79097	2.78566	2.78037
4	3.71710	3.70823	3.69939	3.69059	3.68182	3.67308	3.66438	3.65571	3.64707	3.63847
5	4.57971	4.56666	4.55367	4.54074	4.52787	4.51505	4.50229	4.48959	4.47695	4.46436
6	5.41719	5.39928	5.38146	5.36374	5.34610	5.32855	5.31109	5.29372	5.27644	5.25925
7	6.23028	6.20687	6.18359	6.16044	6.13743	6.11454	6.09179	6.06916	6.04667	6.02430
8	7.01969	6.99017	6.96084	6.93170	6.90274	6.87396	6.84536	6.81694	6.78870	6.76063
9	7.78611	7.74993	7.71400	7.67831	7.64288	7.60769	7.57274	7.53803	7.50356	7.46933
10	8.53020	8.48683	8.44379	8.40108	8.35868	8.31661	8.27484	8.23340	8.19226	8.15142
11	9.25262	9.20159	9.15096	9.10075	9.05095	9.00155	8.95255	8.90395	8.85574	8.80792
12	9.95400	9.89485	9.83620	9.77808	9.72045	9.66333	9.60671	9.55058	9.49493	9.43976
13	10.63496	10.56726	10.50020	10.43376	10.36794	10.30274	10.23814	10.17413	10.11072	10.04790
14	11.29607	11.21946	11.14360	11.06850	10.99414	10.92052	10.84762	10.77544	10.70397	10.63320
15	11.93794	11.85204	11.76706	11.68296	11.59975	11.51741	11.43593	11.35530	11.27550	11.19654
16	12.56110	12.46561	12.37118	12.27780	12.18545	12.09412	12.00379	11.91446	11.82611	11.73873
17	13.16612	13.06073	12.95657	12.85363	12.75188	12.65132	12.55192	12.45368	12.35656	12.26056
18	13.75351	13.63795	13.52381	13.41106	13.29969	13.18968	13.08101	12.97365	12.86759	12.76281
19	14.32380	14.19782	14.07346	13.95069	13.82949	13.70984	13.59171	13.47507	13.35992	13.24621
20	14.87747	14.74085	14.60606	14.47308	14.34187	14.21240	14.08466	13.95861	13.83422	13.71147

Table A-1. (Cont.)

n/r	2.0%	2.1%	2.2%	2.3%	2.4%	2.5%	2.6%	2.7%	2.8%	2.9%
1	.98039	.97943	.97847	.97752	.97656	.97561	.97466	.97371	.97276	.97182
2	1.94156	1.93872	1.93588	1.93306	1.93024	1.92742	1.92462	1.92182	1.91903	1.91625
3	2.88388	2.87828	2.87269	2.86711	2.86156	2.85602	2.85051	2.84501	2.83952	2.83406
4	3.80773	3.79851	3.78932	3.78017	3.77105	3.76197	3.75293	3.74392	3.73494	3.72600
5	4.71346	4.69981	4.68622	4.67270	4.65923	4.64583	4.63248	4.61920	4.60598	4.59281
6	5.60143	5.58258	5.56382	5.54516	5.52659	5.50813	5.48975	5.47147	5.45329	5.43519
7	6.47199	6.44719	6.42252	6.39800	6.37363	6.34939	6.32529	6.30134	6.27751	6.25383
8	7.32548	7.29401	7.26274	7.23168	7.20081	7.17014	7.13966	7.10938	7.07929	7.04940
9	8.16224	8.12342	8.08488	8.04660	8.00860	7.97087	7.93339	7.89619	7.85924	7.82254
10	8.98259	8.93577	8.88931	8.84321	8.79746	8.75206	8.70701	8.66230	8.61793	8.57390
11	9.78685	9.73141	9.67643	9.62191	9.56783	9.51421	9.46103	9.40828	9.35597	9.30408
12	10.57534	10.51068	10.44660	10.38310	10.32015	10.25776	10.19593	10.13464	10.07390	10.01369
13	11.34837	11.27393	11.20020	11.12717	11.05483	10.98318	10.91221	10.84191	10.77227	10.70329
14	12.10625	12.02148	11.93757	11.85452	11.77230	11.69091	11.61034	11.53059	11.45163	11.37346
15	12.84926	12.75365	12.65907	12.56551	12.47295	12.38138	12.29078	12.20116	12.11248	12.02474
16	13.57771	13.47077	13.36504	13.26052	13.15718	13.05500	12.95398	12.85409	12.75533	12.65767
17	14.29187	14.17313	14.05581	13.93990	13.82537	13.71220	13.60037	13.48987	13.38067	13.27276
18	14.99203	14.86105	14.73172	14.60401	14.47790	14.35336	14.23038	14.10893	13.98898	13.87052
19	15.67846	15.53482	15.39307	15.25318	15.11513	14.97889	14.84443	14.71171	14.58072	14.45142
20	16.35143	16.19473	16.04019	15.88777	15.73744	15.58916	15.44291	15.29865	15.15634	15.01596

154

n/r	1.0%	1.1%	1.2%	1.3%	1.4%	1.5%	1.6%	1.7%	1.8%	1.9%
1	.99010	.98912	.98814	.98717	.98619	.98522	.98425	.98328	.98232	.98135
2	1.97040	1.96748	1.96457	1.96167	1.95877	1.95588	1.95300	1.95013	1.94727	1.94441
3	2.94099	2.93519	2.92941	2.92366	2.91792	2.91220	2.90650	2.90082	2.89515	2.88951
4	3.90197	3.89237	3.88282	3.87330	3.86383	3.85438	3.84498	3.83561	3.82628	3.81699
5	4.85343	4.83914	4.82492	4.81076	4.79667	4.78264	4.76868	4.75478	4.74094	4.72717
6	5.79548	5.77561	5.75585	5.73619	5.71664	5.69719	5.67784	5.65859	5.63943	5.62038
7	6.72819	6.70189	6.67574	6.64975	6.62391	6.59821	6.57267	6.54728	6.52204	6.49694
8	7.65168	7.61809	7.58473	7.55158	7.51864	7.48593	7.45342	7.42112	7.38904	7.35716
9	8.56602	8.52432	8.48293	8.44183	8.40103	8.36052	8.32029	8.28036	8.24070	8.20133
10	9.47130	9.42070	9.37048	9.32066	9.27123	9.22218	9.17352	9.12523	9.07731	9.02976
11	10.36763	10.30732	10.24751	10.18822	10.12942	10.07112	10.01330	9.95598	9.89913	9.84275
12	11.25508	11.18429	11.11414	11.04464	10.97576	10.90751	10.83987	10.77284	10.70641	10.64058
13	12.13374	12.05172	11.97050	11.89007	11.81041	11.73153	11.65341	11.57604	11.49942	11.42353
14	13.00370	12.90971	12.81670	12.72465	12.63354	12.54338	12.45415	12.36583	12.27841	12.19189
15	13.86505	13.75837	13.65286	13.54852	13.44531	13.34323	13.24227	13.14241	13.04363	12.94592
16	14.71787	14.59780	14.47911	14.36181	14.24587	14.13126	14.01798	13.90600	13.79531	13.68588
17	15.56225	15.42809	15.29557	15.16467	15.03537	14.90765	14.78148	14.65684	14.53370	14.41206
18	16.39827	16.24934	16.10234	15.95723	15.81398	15.67256	15.53295	15.39512	15.25904	15.12469
19	17.22601	17.06167	16.89955	16.73961	16.58183	16.42617	16.27259	16.12106	15.97155	15.82403
20	18.04555	17.86515	17.68730	17.51196	17.33908	17.16864	17.00058	16.83487	16.67147	16.51033

Notes to Table A–2

Table A-2 gives the present value of $1.00 payable in some future period at a given discount rate. For example, the present value of $1.00 payable at the end of 10 periods, discounted at 6 percent, equals $1.00 × .5584, or 56 cents.

In the illustrating problems used in the various chapters, the table readings are rounded to three places. Thus .5584 becomes .558. See note to Table A-1.

Figure A–2.   Graphic Illustration of Present Value
Calculations at 4% Interest

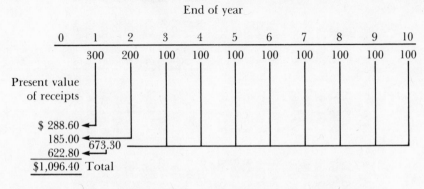

Reprinted with permission of the American College, Bryn Mawr.

Table A–2. Present Value of $1.00

n/r	36%	37%	38%	39%	40%	41%	42%	43%	44%	45%	46%	47%	48%
1	0.7353	0.7299	0.7246	0.7194	0.7143	0.7092	0.7042	0.6993	0.6944	0.6897	0.6849	0.6803	0.6757
2	0.5407	0.5328	0.5251	0.5176	0.5102	0.5030	0.4959	0.4890	0.4823	0.4756	0.4691	0.4628	0.4565
3	0.3975	0.3889	0.3805	0.3724	0.3644	0.3567	0.3492	0.3420	0.3349	0.3280	0.3213	0.3148	0.3085
4	0.2923	0.2839	0.2757	0.2679	0.2603	0.2530	0.2459	0.2391	0.2326	0.2262	0.2201	0.2142	0.2084
5	0.2149	0.2072	0.1998	0.1927	0.1859	0.1794	0.1732	0.1672	0.1615	0.1560	0.1507	0.1457	0.1408
6	0.1580	0.1512	0.1448	0.1386	0.1328	0.1273	0.1220	0.1169	0.1122	0.1076	0.1032	0.0991	0.0952
7	0.1162	0.1104	0.1049	0.0997	0.0949	0.0903	0.0859	0.0818	0.0779	0.0742	0.0707	0.0674	0.0643
8	0.0854	0.0806	0.0760	0.0718	0.0678	0.0640	0.0605	0.0572	0.0541	0.0512	0.0484	0.0459	0.0434
9	0.0628	0.0588	0.0551	0.0516	0.0484	0.0454	0.0426	0.0400	0.0376	0.0353	0.0332	0.0312	0.0294
10	0.0462	0.0429	0.0399	0.0371	0.0346	0.0322	0.0300	0.0280	0.0261	0.0243	0.0227	0.0212	0.0198
11	0.0340	0.0313	0.0289	0.0267	0.0247	0.0228	0.0211	0.0196	0.0181	0.0168	0.0156	0.0144	0.0134
12	0.0250	0.0229	0.0210	0.0192	0.0176	0.0162	0.0149	0.0137	0.0126	0.0116	0.0107	0.0098	0.0091
13	0.0184	0.0167	0.0152	0.0138	0.0126	0.0115	0.0105	0.0096	0.0087	0.0080	0.0073	0.0067	0.0061
14	0.0135	0.0122	0.0110	0.0099	0.0090	0.0081	0.0074	0.0067	0.0061	0.0055	0.0050	0.0045	0.0041
15	0.0099	0.0089	0.0080	0.0072	0.0064	0.0058	0.0052	0.0047	0.0042	0.0038	0.0034	0.0031	0.0028
16	0.0073	0.0065	0.0058	0.0051	0.0046	0.0041	0.0037	0.0033	0.0029	0.0026	0.0023	0.0021	0.0019
17	0.0054	0.0047	0.0042	0.0037	0.0033	0.0029	0.0026	0.0023	0.0020	0.0018	0.0016	0.0014	0.0013
18	0.0039	0.0035	0.0030	0.0027	0.0023	0.0021	0.0018	0.0016	0.0014	0.0012	0.0011	0.0010	0.0009
19	0.0029	0.0025	0.0022	0.0019	0.0017	0.0015	0.0013	0.0011	0.0010	0.0009	0.0008	0.0007	0.0006
20	0.0021	0.0018	0.0016	0.0014	0.0012	0.0010	0.0009	0.0008	0.0007	0.0006	0.0005	0.0005	0.0004

n = number of time periods; r = rate of interest in percent.

Table A–2. (Cont.)

n/r	26%	27%	28%	29%	30%	31%	32%	33%	34%	35%
1	0.7937	0.7874	0.7813	0.7752	0.7692	0.7634	0.7576	0.7519	0.7463	0.7407
2	0.6299	0.6200	0.6104	0.6009	0.5917	0.5827	0.5739	0.5653	0.5569	0.5487
3	0.4999	0.4882	0.4768	0.4658	0.4552	0.4448	0.4348	0.4251	0.4156	0.4064
4	0.3968	0.3844	0.3725	0.3611	0.3501	0.3396	0.3294	0.3196	0.3102	0.3011
5	0.3149	0.3027	0.2910	0.2799	0.2693	0.2592	0.2495	0.2403	0.2315	0.2230
6	0.2499	0.2383	0.2274	0.2170	0.2072	0.1979	0.1890	0.1807	0.1727	0.1652
7	0.1983	0.1877	0.1776	0.1682	0.1594	0.1510	0.1432	0.1358	0.1289	0.1224
8	0.1574	0.1478	0.1388	0.1304	0.1226	0.1153	0.1085	0.1021	0.0962	0.0906
9	0.1249	0.1164	0.1084	0.1011	0.0943	0.0880	0.0822	0.0768	0.0718	0.0671
10	0.0992	0.0916	0.0847	0.0784	0.0725	0.0672	0.0623	0.0577	0.0536	0.0497
11	0.0787	0.0721	0.0662	0.0607	0.0558	0.0513	0.0472	0.0434	0.0400	0.0368
12	0.0625	0.0568	0.0517	0.0471	0.0429	0.0392	0.0357	0.0326	0.0298	0.0273
13	0.0496	0.0447	0.0404	0.0365	0.0330	0.0299	0.0271	0.0245	0.0223	0.0202
14	0.0393	0.0352	0.0316	0.0283	0.0253	0.0228	0.0205	0.0185	0.0166	0.0150
15	0.0312	0.0277	0.0247	0.0219	0.0195	0.0174	0.0155	0.0139	0.0124	0.0111
16	0.0248	0.0218	0.0193	0.0170	0.0150	0.0133	0.0118	0.0104	0.0093	0.0082
17	0.0197	0.0172	0.0150	0.0132	0.0116	0.0101	0.0089	0.0078	0.0069	0.0061
18	0.0156	0.0135	0.0118	0.0102	0.0089	0.0077	0.0068	0.0059	0.0052	0.0045
19	0.0124	0.0107	0.0092	0.0079	0.0068	0.0059	0.0051	0.0044	0.0038	0.0033
20	0.0098	0.0084	0.0072	0.0061	0.0053	0.0045	0.0039	0.0033	0.0029	0.0025

n/r	16%	17%	18%	19%	20%	21%	22%	23%	24%	25%
1	0.8621	0.8547	0.8475	0.8403	0.8333	0.8264	0.8197	0.8130	0.8065	0.8000
2	0.7432	0.7305	0.7182	0.7062	0.6944	0.6830	0.6719	0.6610	0.6504	0.6400
3	0.6407	0.6244	0.6086	0.5934	0.5787	0.5645	0.5507	0.5374	0.5245	0.5120
4	0.5523	0.5337	0.5158	0.4987	0.4823	0.4665	0.4514	0.4369	0.4230	0.4096
5	0.4761	0.4561	0.4371	0.4190	0.4019	0.3855	0.3700	0.3552	0.3411	0.3277
6	0.4104	0.3898	0.3704	0.3521	0.3349	0.3186	0.3033	0.2888	0.2751	0.2621
7	0.3538	0.3332	0.3139	0.2959	0.2791	0.2633	0.2486	0.2348	0.2218	0.2097
8	0.3050	0.2848	0.2660	0.2487	0.2326	0.2176	0.2038	0.1909	0.1789	0.1678
9	0.2630	0.2434	0.2255	0.2090	0.1938	0.1799	0.1670	0.1552	0.1443	0.1342
10	0.2267	0.2080	0.1911	0.1756	0.1615	0.1486	0.1369	0.1262	0.1164	0.1074
11	0.1954	0.1778	0.1619	0.1476	0.1346	0.1228	0.1122	0.1026	0.0938	0.0859
12	0.1685	0.1520	0.1372	0.1240	0.1122	0.1015	0.0920	0.0834	0.0757	0.0687
13	0.1452	0.1299	0.1163	0.1042	0.0935	0.0839	0.0754	0.0678	0.0610	0.0550
14	0.1252	0.1110	0.0985	0.0876	0.0779	0.0693	0.0618	0.0551	0.0492	0.0440
15	0.1079	0.0949	0.0835	0.0736	0.0649	0.0573	0.0507	0.0448	0.0397	0.0352
16	0.0930	0.0811	0.0708	0.0618	0.0541	0.0474	0.0415	0.0364	0.0320	0.0281
17	0.0802	0.0693	0.0600	0.0520	0.0451	0.0391	0.0340	0.0296	0.0258	0.0225
18	0.0691	0.0592	0.0508	0.0437	0.0376	0.0323	0.0279	0.0241	0.0208	0.0180
19	0.0596	0.0506	0.0431	0.0367	0.0313	0.0267	0.0229	0.0196	0.0168	0.0144
20	0.0514	0.0433	0.0365	0.0308	0.0261	0.0221	0.0187	0.0159	0.0135	0.0115

Table A-2. (Cont.)

n/r	6%	7%	8%	9%	10%	11%	12%	13%	14%	15%
1	0.9434	0.9346	0.9259	0.9174	0.9091	0.9009	0.8929	0.8850	0.8772	0.8696
2	0.8900	0.8734	0.8573	0.8417	0.8264	0.8116	0.7972	0.7831	0.7695	0.7561
3	0.8396	0.8163	0.7938	0.7722	0.7513	0.7312	0.7118	0.6931	0.6750	0.6575
4	0.7921	0.7629	0.7350	0.7084	0.6830	0.6587	0.6355	0.6133	0.5921	0.5718
5	0.7473	0.7130	0.6806	0.6499	0.6209	0.5935	0.5674	0.5428	0.5194	0.4972
6	0.7050	0.6663	0.6302	0.5963	0.5645	0.5346	0.5066	0.4803	0.4556	0.4323
7	0.6651	0.6227	0.5835	0.5470	0.5132	0.4817	0.4523	0.4251	0.3996	0.3759
8	0.6274	0.5820	0.5403	0.5019	0.4665	0.4339	0.4039	0.3762	0.3506	0.3269
9	0.5919	0.5439	0.5002	0.4604	0.4241	0.3909	0.3606	0.3329	0.3075	0.2843
10	0.5584	0.5083	0.4632	0.4224	0.3855	0.3522	0.3220	0.2946	0.2697	0.2472
11	0.5268	0.4751	0.4289	0.3875	0.3505	0.3173	0.2875	0.2607	0.2366	0.2149
12	0.4970	0.4440	0.3971	0.3555	0.3186	0.2858	0.2567	0.2307	0.2076	0.1869
13	0.4688	0.4150	0.3677	0.3262	0.2897	0.2575	0.2292	0.2042	0.1821	0.1625
14	0.4423	0.3878	0.3405	0.2992	0.2633	0.2320	0.2046	0.1807	0.1597	0.1413
15	0.4173	0.3624	0.3152	0.2745	0.2394	0.2090	0.1827	0.1599	0.1401	0.1229
16	0.3936	0.3387	0.2919	0.2519	0.2176	0.1883	0.1631	0.1415	0.1229	0.1069
17	0.3714	0.3166	0.2703	0.2311	0.1978	0.1696	0.1456	0.1252	0.1078	0.0929
18	0.3503	0.2959	0.2502	0.2120	0.1799	0.1528	0.1300	0.1108	0.0946	0.0808
19	0.3305	0.2765	0.2317	0.1945	0.1635	0.1377	0.1161	0.0981	0.0829	0.0703
20	0.3118	0.2584	0.2145	0.1784	0.1486	0.1240	0.1037	0.0868	0.0728	0.0611

n/r	5.0%	5.1%	5.2%	5.3%	5.4%	5.5%	5.6%	5.7%	5.8%	5.9%
1	.952381	.951475	.950570	.949668	.948767	.947867	.946970	.946074	.945180	.944287
2	.907029	.905304	.903584	.901869	.900158	.898452	.896752	.895056	.893364	.891678
3	.863838	.861374	.858920	.856475	.854040	.851614	.849197	.846789	.844390	.842000
4	.822702	.819576	.816464	.813367	.810285	.807217	.804163	.801125	.798100	.795090
5	.783526	.779806	.776106	.772428	.768771	.765134	.761518	.757923	.754348	.750793
6	.746215	.741965	.737744	.733550	.729384	.725246	.721135	.717051	.712994	.708964
7	.710681	.705961	.701277	.696629	.692015	.687437	.682893	.678383	.673908	.669466
8	.676839	.671705	.666613	.661566	.656561	.651599	.646679	.641801	.636964	.632168
9	.644609	.639110	.633663	.628268	.622923	.617629	.612385	.607191	.602045	.596948
10	.613913	.608097	.602341	.596645	.591009	.585431	.579910	.574447	.569041	.563690
11	.584679	.578589	.572568	.566615	.560729	.554911	.549157	.543469	.537846	.532285
12	.556837	.550513	.544266	.538096	.532001	.525982	.520035	.514162	.508361	.502630
13	.530321	.523799	.517363	.511012	.504745	.498561	.492458	.486435	.480492	.474627
14	.505068	.498382	.491790	.485292	.478885	.472569	.466343	.460204	.454151	.448184
15	.481017	.474197	.467481	.460866	.454350	.447933	.441612	.435387	.429255	.423215
16	.458112	.451187	.444374	.437669	.431072	.424581	.418194	.411908	.405723	.399636
17	.436297	.429293	.422408	.415640	.408987	.402447	.396017	.389695	.383458	.377371
18	.415521	.408461	.401529	.394720	.388033	.381466	.375016	.368681	.362458	.356347
19	.395734	.388641	.381681	.374853	.368153	.361579	.355129	.348799	.342588	.336494
20	.376889	.369782	.362815	.355986	.349291	.342729	.336296	.329990	.323807	.317747

Table A-2. (Cont.)

n/r	4.0%	4.1%	4.2%	4.3%	4.4%	4.5%	4.6%	4.7%	4.8%	4.9%
1	.961538	.960615	.959693	.958773	.957854	.956938	.956023	.955110	.954198	.953289
2	.924556	.922781	.921010	.919245	.917485	.915730	.913980	.912235	.910495	.908760
3	.888996	.886437	.883887	.881347	.878817	.876297	.873786	.871284	.868793	.866310
4	.854804	.851524	.848260	.845012	.841779	.838561	.835359	.832172	.829001	.825844
5	.821927	.817987	.814069	.810174	.806302	.802451	.798623	.794816	.791031	.787268
6	.790315	.785770	.781257	.776773	.772320	.767896	.763501	.759137	.754801	.750494
7	.759918	.754823	.749766	.744749	.739770	.734828	.729925	.725059	.720230	.715437
8	.730690	.725094	.719545	.714045	.708592	.703185	.697825	.692511	.687242	.682018
9	.702587	.696536	.690543	.684607	.678728	.672904	.667137	.661424	.655765	.650161
10	.675564	.669103	.662709	.656382	.650122	.643928	.637798	.631732	.625730	.619791
11	.649581	.642750	.635997	.629322	.622722	.616199	.609750	.603374	.597071	.590840
12	.624597	.617435	.610362	.603376	.596477	.589664	.582935	.576288	.569724	.563241
13	.600574	.593117	.585760	.578501	.571339	.564272	.557299	.550419	.543630	.536931
14	.577475	.569757	.562150	.554651	.547259	.539973	.532790	.525710	.518731	.511851
15	.555265	.547317	.539491	.531784	.524195	.516720	.509360	.502111	.494972	.487941
16	.533908	.525761	.517746	.509860	.502102	.494469	.486960	.479571	.472302	.465149
17	.513373	.505054	.496877	.488840	.480941	.473176	.465545	.458043	.450670	.443421
18	.493628	.485162	.476849	.468687	.460671	.452800	.445071	.437482	.430028	.422709
19	.474642	.466054	.457629	.449364	.441256	.433302	.425498	.417843	.410332	.402964
20	.456387	.447698	.439183	.430838	.422659	.414643	.406786	.399086	.391538	.384141

n/r	3.0%	3.1%	3.2%	3.3%	3.4%	3.5%	3.6%	3.7%	3.8%	3.9%
1	.970874	.969932	.968992	.968054	.967118	.966184	.965251	.964320	.963391	.962464
2	.942596	.940768	.938946	.937129	.935317	.933511	.931709	.929913	.928122	.926337
3	.915142	.912481	.909831	.907192	.904562	.901943	.899333	.896734	.894145	.891566
4	.888487	.885045	.881620	.878211	.874818	.871442	.868082	.864739	.861411	.858100
5	.862609	.858434	.854283	.850156	.846052	.841973	.837917	.833885	.829876	.825890
6	.837484	.832622	.827793	.822997	.818233	.813501	.808801	.804132	.799495	.794889
7	.813092	.807587	.802125	.796705	.791327	.785991	.780696	.775441	.770227	.765052
8	.789409	.783305	.777253	.771254	.765307	.759412	.753567	.747773	.742030	.736335
9	.766417	.759752	.753152	.746616	.740142	.733731	.727381	.721093	.714865	.708696
10	.744094	.736908	.729799	.722764	.715805	.708919	.702106	.695364	.688694	.682094
11	.722421	.714751	.707169	.699675	.692268	.684946	.677708	.670554	.663482	.656491
12	.701380	.693260	.685241	.677323	.669505	.661783	.654158	.646629	.639193	.631849
13	.680951	.672415	.663994	.655686	.647490	.639404	.631427	.623557	.615793	.608132
14	.661118	.652197	.643405	.634739	.626199	.617782	.609486	.601309	.593249	.585305
15	.641862	.632587	.623454	.614462	.605608	.596891	.588307	.579854	.571531	.563335
16	.623167	.613566	.604122	.594833	.585695	.576706	.567863	.559165	.550608	.542190
17	.605016	.595117	.585390	.575830	.566436	.557204	.548131	.539214	.530451	.521838
18	.587395	.577224	.567238	.557435	.547810	.538361	.529084	.519975	.511031	.502250
19	.570286	.559868	.549649	.539627	.529797	.520156	.510699	.501422	.492323	.483398
20	.553676	.543034	.532606	.522388	.512377	.502566	.492952	.483532	.474300	.465253

Table A–2. (Cont.)

n/r	2.0%	2.1%	2.2%	2.3%	2.4%	2.5%	2.6%	2.7%	2.8%	2.9%
1	.980392	.979432	.978474	.977517	.976562	.975610	.974659	.973710	.972763	.971817
2	.961169	.959287	.957411	.955540	.953674	.951814	.949960	.948111	.946267	.944429
3	.942322	.939556	.936801	.934056	.931323	.928599	.925887	.923185	.920493	.917812
4	.923845	.920231	.916635	.913056	.909495	.905951	.902424	.898914	.895422	.891946
5	.905731	.901304	.896903	.892528	.888178	.883854	.879555	.875282	.871033	.866808
6	.887971	.882766	.877596	.872461	.867362	.862297	.857266	.852270	.847308	.842379
7	.870560	.864609	.858704	.852846	.847033	.841265	.835542	.829864	.824230	.818639
8	.853490	.846826	.840220	.833671	.827181	.820747	.814369	.808047	.801780	.795567
9	.836755	.829408	.822133	.814928	.807794	.800728	.793732	.786803	.779941	.773146
10	.820348	.812349	.804435	.796606	.788861	.781198	.773618	.766118	.758698	.751357
11	.804263	.795640	.787119	.778696	.770372	.762145	.754013	.745976	.738033	.730182
12	.788493	.779276	.770175	.761189	.752316	.743556	.734906	.726365	.717931	.709603
13	.773033	.763247	.753596	.744075	.734684	.725420	.716282	.707268	.698376	.689605
14	.757875	.747549	.737373	.727346	.717465	.707727	.698131	.688674	.679354	.670170
15	.743015	.732173	.721500	.710993	.700649	.690466	.680440	.670569	.660851	.651282
16	.728446	.717114	.705969	.695008	.684228	.673625	.663197	.652939	.642851	.632928
17	.714163	.702364	.690772	.679382	.668191	.657195	.646390	.635774	.625341	.615090
18	.700159	.687918	.675902	.664108	.652530	.641166	.630010	.619059	.608309	.597755
19	.686431	.673769	.661352	.649177	.637237	.625528	.614045	.602784	.591740	.580909
20	.672971	.659911	.647116	.634581	.622302	.610271	.598484	.586937	.575622	.564537

n/r	1.0%	1.1%	1.2%	1.3%	1.4%	1.5%	1.6%	1.7%	1.8%	1.9%
1	.990099	.989120	.988142	.987167	.986193	.985222	.984252	.983284	.982318	.981354
2	.980296	.978358	.976425	.974498	.972577	.970662	.968752	.966848	.964949	.963056
3	.970590	.967713	.964847	.961992	.959149	.956317	.953496	.950686	.947887	.945099
4	.960980	.957184	.953406	.949647	.945906	.942184	.938480	.934795	.931127	.927477
5	.951466	.946769	.942101	.937460	.932847	.928260	.923701	.919169	.914663	.910184
6	.942045	.936468	.930930	.925429	.919967	.914542	.909155	.903804	.898490	.893213
7	.932718	.926279	.919891	.913553	.907265	.901027	.894837	.888696	.882603	.876558
8	.923483	.916201	.908983	.901829	.894739	.887711	.880745	.873841	.866997	.860214
9	.914340	.906232	.898205	.890256	.882386	.874592	.866875	.859234	.851667	.844175
10	.905287	.896372	.887554	.878831	.870203	.861667	.853224	.844871	.836608	.828434
11	.896324	.886620	.877030	.867553	.858188	.848933	.839787	.830748	.821816	.812988
12	.887449	.876973	.866630	.856420	.846339	.836387	.826562	.816862	.807285	.797829
13	.878663	.867431	.856354	.845429	.834654	.824027	.813545	.803207	.793010	.782953
14	.869963	.857993	.846200	.834580	.823130	.811849	.800734	.789781	.778989	.768354
15	.861349	.848658	.836166	.823869	.811766	.799852	.788124	.776579	.765215	.754028
16	.852821	.839424	.826251	.813296	.800558	.788031	.775712	.763598	.751684	.739968
17	.844377	.830291	.816453	.802859	.789505	.776385	.763496	.750834	.738393	.726171
18	.836017	.821257	.806772	.792556	.778604	.764912	.751473	.738283	.725337	.712631
19	.827740	.812322	.797205	.782385	.767854	.753607	.739639	.725942	.712512	.699343
20	.819544	.803483	.787752	.772345	.757253	.742470	.727991	.713807	.699914	.686304

Bibliography

"Alaska Booms and Hassles Reported by Rental Operations," *Rent Equipment* (September 1975), p. 22.

"Auto Repair Products Rental Possibilities Explored," *Rent All* (July 1975), p. 25.

"Banks Cash In on Capital Equipment Leasing Business," *Business Week* (August 8, 1977), p. 62.

"California: Spark Arrestors on Internal Combustion Equipment are Required, Renter Can be Held Liable," *Rent Equipment* (June 1977), p. 61.

"Car and Truck Lease — Rental Registration for 1974-76," *Ward's Auto Reports* (February 20, 1978), p. 60.

"Citicorp — Machine Tool Leasing Drive Stepped-Up," *American Metal Market*, (March 17, 1975), p. 10.

"Commerce Department Says 1,400 Banks, Bank Holding Companies are Active in Leasing," *American Banker* (December 23, 1976), p. 2.

"Construction and Industrial Equipment Rental Market Survey and Analysis," *Rent All* (March 1977), p. 20.

"Construction Machinery Rentals Data, 1979," *Engineering News* (March 22, 1979), p. 101.

"Consumer Leasing and Renting As a Marketing Alternative Discussed," *Business Horizon* (October 1976), p. 82.

"Contractor Rental Firm Eases Recession Pain via Tight Ship," *Rent Equipment* (June 1975), p. 25.

"Describes Development in Aviation Lease Market," *Interavia* (December 1978), p. 1194.

"Directory of Manufacturers and Distributors of Items For Rental Operations Including Addresses and Phone Numbers," *Rent Equipment*, (June 1977), p. 58A.

167

"Discusses Advantages of Truck Leasing for Oil Marketers," *N. P. News* (February 1979), p. 49.

"Discusses Equipment Leasing v. Purchase and IRS Rules, Types of Leases and Cost Consideration," *Tire Dealer* (November 1978), P.R1.

"Discusses Over $100 Million Electronics Rental Market and Future Trends in this Market," *Electrical Engineering* (October 30, 1978), p. 37.

"Discusses Relationship of Rental Rates and Rental Industry Growth," *Rent Equipment* (June 1977), p. 77.

"Economics of Buying, Leasing and Renting Construction Equipment Compared," *Engineering News* (February 6, 1975), p. 39.

"Equipment Lease Financing Variations Explored," *Iron Age* (August 8, 1975), p. 35.

"Equipment Leasing Market Expected to Reach $42-$43 Billion by 1982," *Purchasing* (January 1979), p. 38.

"Examines Tax Advantages and Disadvantages in Leasing Trucks and Cars," *R&P News* (February 5, 1979), p. 4.

"Financial Appraisal of the Leasing Industry," *Value Line* (April 1, 1975), p. 214.

"Forecasts Medical and Dental Equipment Market and Inventory of Capital Equipment Out on Lease," *Medical Digest* (August 8, 1976), p. 3.

"Gel Co. — Profile Auto and Equipment Leasing Company," *Forbes* (November 1, 1976), p. 77.

"Hertz — Says Truck Leasing Saves Energy and Dollars," *Journal of Commerce* (May 29, 1979), p. 2.

"High Auto Prices Spur Leasing Boom," *New York Times* (February 17, 1979) p. L27.

"How to Solve Weekend Overload of Equipment Rentals: Use Discount Plan," *Rent Equipment* (December 1976), p. 29.

"Leasing Equipment is Mystery to Both Farmers and Bankers," *American Banker* (July 3, 1975), p. 6.

"Leasing Industry Revenues Projected, 1980," *Fortune* (November 1976), p. 50.

"Leasing Market of Industrial Equipment Seen Booming," *Iron Age* (October 10, 1977), p. 33.

"A Look at How Inflation Hurts Rental Business," *Rent All* (February 1977), p. 15.

"Motor Vehicle Rent and Lease Revenues Data, 1978," *U. S. Outlook* (January 1978), p. 450.

"Motor Vehicle Rent and Lease Revenues Data, 1979," *U. S. Outlook* (January 1979), p. 495.

"1974, Instrument Leasing Markets, By Bype," *Electric News* (October 13, 1975), p. 52.

"Offers Tips on Effective Rental of Medical Equipment," *Rent All* (January 1979), p. 16.

"Outlook for Medical, Exercise and Guest Room Equipment Sales and Rental Including Outlet Survey," *Rent All* (August 1975), p. 21.

"The Powerful Logic of the Leasing Boom," Peter Vanderwicken, *Fortune* (November 1973), p. 132.

"Presents Pros and Cons of Renting Linen," *Linen News* (March 1979), p. 38.

"Rental Operators Surveyed on Importance of Sales to Business," *Rent All* (June 1975), p. 23.

"Role of Long Term Pacts in Future of Rental Business Discussed," *Rent Equipment* (July 1975), p. 9.

"Sea Container Vies with CTI in Container Leasing," *Financial Times* (October 26, 1977), p. 27.

"Separate Personal and Business Uses of Company Cars for Tax Purposes; Leasing May Solve Problems," *Auto News* (October 9, 1978), p. 12.

"Survey Finds Price Not Major Factor in Auto Rental Decisions," *Journal of Commerce*, (August 31, 1976), p. 2.

"U.S. Leasing International Examines New Policy of Harvesting Investments: Possible 50% Yield," *Business Week*, (December 4, 1978), p. 108.

Lease Evaluation Articles

BATKIN, ALAN, "Leasing vs. Buying: A Guide for the Perplexed," *Financial Executive*, 41 (June 1973), 63-68.

BEECHY, THOMAS H., "The Cost of Leasing: Comment and Correction," *Accounting Review*, 45 (October 1970), 769-73.

————, "Quasi-Debt Analysis of Financial Leases," *Accounting Review*, 44 (April 1969), 375-81.

Bower, Richard S., "Issues In Lease Financing" (1974) (unpublished mimeo).

———, Frank C. Herringer, and J. Peter Williamson, "Lease Evaluation," *Accounting Review*, 41 (April 1966), 257-65.

Chasteen, Lanny G., "Implicit Factors in the Evaluation of Lease vs. Buy Alternatives," *Accounting Review*, 48 (October 1973), 764-67.

Ferrara, William L., "Capital Budgeting and Financing or Leasing Decision," *Management Accounting*, 49 (July 1968), 55-63.

———, "Lease vs. Purchase: A Quasi-Financing Approach," *Management Accounting*, 56 (January 1974), 21-26.

———, "Should Investment and Financing Decisions Be Separated?" *Accounting Review*, 41 (January 1966), 106-14.

Gant, Donald R., "A Critical Look at Lease Financing," *Controller*, 29 (June 1961), 274-77, 311-12.

———, "Illusion in Lease Financing," *Harvard Business Review*, 37 (March-April 1959), 121-42.

Gaumnitz, Jack E., and Allen Ford, "The Lease or Sell Decision," *Financial Management* (Winter 1978), 69-74.

Gordon, Myron J., "A General Solution to the Buy or Lease Decision: A Pedogogical Note," *Journal of Finance*, 29 (March 1974), 245-50.

Griesinger, Frank K., "Pros and Cons of Leasing Equipment," *Harvard Business Review*, 33 (March-April 1955), 75-89.

Hamel, H. G., *Leasing in Industry*. New York: National Industrial Conference Board, 1968.

Hawkins, David F., and Mary M. Wehle, *Accounting for Leases*. New York: Financial Executives Research Foundation, 1973.

Johnson, R. W., and W. G. Lewellen, "Analysis of the Lease or Buy Decision," *Journal of Finance*, 27 (September 1972), 815-23.

Knutson, Peter H., "Leased Equipment and Divisional Return on Capital," *N.A.A. Bulletin*, 44 (November 1962), 15-20.

MacEachron, William, D., "Leasing: A Discounted Cash-Flow Approach," *Controller*, 29 (May 1961), 213-19.

McLean, James H., "Economic and Accounting Aspects of Lease Financing," *Financial Executive*, 31 (December 1963), 18-23.

Mitchell, G. B., "After-Tax Cost of Leasing," *Accounting Review*, 45 (April 1970), 308-14.

PARKER, GEORGE G. C., "The Lease: Use without Ownership," *Columbia Journal of World Business*, 5 (September–October 1970), 77–82.

REILLY, FRANK, "A Direct Cost Lease Evaluation Method," *Bank Administration* (July 1972), 22–26.

SAX, FRANKLIN S., "Lease or Purchase Decision: Present Value Method," *Management Accounting*, 47 (October 1965), 55–61.

THULIN, W. BERNARD, "Own or Lease: Underlying Financial Theory," *Financial Executive*, 32 (April 1964), 23–24, 28–31.

VANCIL, RICHARD F., "Lease or Borrow: New Method of Analysis," *Harvard Business Review*, 39 (September–October 1961), 122–36.

_____, "Lease or Borrow: Steps in Negotiation," *Harvard Business Review*, 39 (November–December 1961), 138–59.

_____, AND ROBERT N. ANTHONY, "The Financial Community Looks at Leasing," *Harvard Business Review*, 37 (November–December 1959), 113–30.

WILSON, CHARLES J., "The Operating Lease and the Risk of Obsolescence," *Management Accounting*, 55 (December 1973), 41–44.

WYMAN, HAROLD E., "Financial Lease Evaluation under Conditions of Uncertainty," *Accounting Review*, 48 (July 1973), 489–93.

ZISES, ALVIN, "Lease Financing: A Reply," *Controller*, 29 (September 1961), 414–23.

Index